Why Me?

by the same author

Are You Okay?
A Practical Guide to Helping Young Victims of Crime
Pete Wallis
ISBN 978 1 84905 098 2

What Have I Done?
A Victim Empathy Programme for Young People
Pete Wallis with Clair Aldington and Marian Liebmann
Illustrated by Emily Wallis
ISBN 978 1 84310 979 2

The Pocket Guide to Restorative Justice
Pete Wallis and Barbara Tudor
ISBN 978 1 84310 629 6

of related interest

Restorative Justice
How it Works
Marian Liebmann
ISBN 978 1 84310 074 4

Cyberbullying
Activities to Help Children and Teens to Stay Safe in a Texting, Twittering, Social Networking World
Vanessa Rogers
ISBN 978 184905 105 7

Youth Offending and Youth Justice
Edited by Monica Barry and Fergus McNeill
ISBN 978 1 84310 689 0
Research Highlights in Social Work Series

Just Care
Restorative Justice Approaches to Working with Children in Public Care
Belinda Hopkins
Foreword by Jonathan Stanley
ISBN 978 1 84310 132 1

Working with Anger and Young People
Nick Luxmoore
ISBN 978 1 84310 466 7

Why Me?

A Programme for Children and Young People Who Have Experienced Victimization

Shellie Keen, Tracey Lott and Pete Wallis

Jessica Kingsley *Publishers*
London and Philadelphia

The Blob Tree is from *Games Without Frontiers* by Pip Wilson © Pip Wilson and Ian Long and is reproduced with permission from Pip Wilson.

First published in 2010
by Jessica Kingsley Publishers
116 Pentonville Road
London N1 9JB, UK
and
400 Market Street, Suite 400
Philadelphia, PA 19106, USA
www.jkp.com

Copyright © Shellie Keen, Tracey Lott, Pete Wallis and Oxfordshire County Council 2010
Illustrations copyright © Nick Mussell 2010
Cover illustration by Emily Milne Wallis

Library of Congress Cataloging in Publication Data
Keen, Shellie, 1972-
  Why me? : a programme for children and young people who have experienced victimization / Shellie Keen, Tracey Lott and Pete Wallis.
     p. cm.
   ISBN 978-1-84905-097-5 (alk. paper)
  1. Victims of crimes--Psychology. 2. Abused children--Services for. 3. Youth-
-Services for. I. Lott, Tracey, 1972- II. Wallis, Pete. III. Title.

   HV6250.25.K44 2010
   362.88--dc22
                              2010009686

British Library Cataloguing in Publication Data
A CIP catalogue record for this book is available from the British Library

ISBN 978 1 84905 097 5

Printed and bound in Great Britain by
MPG Books Group

Contents

Section III: Further Resources

List of handouts

Preface

Reducing crime and improving the justice system is a central part of the Government's effort to build safer communities and to drive down crime. Crime can have devastating consequences for victims and their families, and it is therefore important that support is available that meets individuals' needs.

The Youth Crime Action Plan (YCAP), a cross-Government initiative, was published in July 2008. The plan sets out a triple-track approach of enforcement and punishment, support and prevention. The YCAP contains a chapter dedicated to supporting young people who are victims of crime and to improving support for young witnesses to attend court. One of the commitments made in this chapter is to pilot innovative ways to support young people experiencing victimization and to ensure good practice is taken forward. Since December 2008, five pilot projects have been testing a number of initiatives to improve support for young people who have been victims of crime.

This resource and its sister publication *Are You Okay? A Practical Guide to Helping Young Victims of Crime* by Pete Wallis (also published by Jessica Kingsley Publishers) were produced by the Oxfordshire Young Victims of Crime Project, which is one of the five pilots. The materials contained within *Why Me?* have been tried and tested by specially selected project support staff drawn from a variety of backgrounds including victim support, youth offending, youth service, police and school counselling. They were recruited to deliver the materials on an individual basis to young people who had experienced victimization, over a course of up to six sessions. The materials within this resource have been developed to reflect both the needs of the supporting adults and those of the young people experiencing victimization.

Acknowledgements

This resource was compiled by Shellie Keen, Tracey Lott and Pete Wallis on behalf of the Oxfordshire Young Victims of Crime Project Consortium, which comprises Oxfordshire Youth Offending Service, Victim Support, Thames Valley Partnership, Thames Valley Police (Youth Justice), Oxfordshire Youth Support Services, Bartholomew School, Meadowbrook School, Oxford School, Iffley Mead School, Oxfordshire Witness Care Unit, Crown Prosecution Service Youth Specialist, Oxfordshire Safer Communities, and Oxfordshire County Council Domestic Violence and Anti-bullying Co-ordinators and Participation and Play lead.

It has been a truly collaborative venture with contributions from colleagues and experts in many different fields who have generously offered their time to check the content for accuracy, and to contribute case studies and many lovely creative ideas.

Huge thanks to the following: The Oxfordshire Young Victims of Crime Project support workers – namely, Colette Selwood, Janice Nicholls, Jane Fangman, Lorraine Lock, Mark Sainsbury, Mark Webb, Rebecca Harvey, Simon Edmondson, Sophie Phipps and Vicki Causer; all the staff and management at Oxfordshire Youth Offending Service, particularly Gordon Richardson, Tan Lea, Joseph Nwokobia and Sue Howarth; all the young people who were involved in the pilot, and their families; Jake Greenwood, Nigel Mayer, Kirsty Scott and Gita Sisupalan at the Office for Criminal Justice Reform; the Oxfordshire County Council Young People's Sounding Board; Source Workers who are young people in care or leaving the care of the local authority; students at Meadowbrook College; Oxfordshire's Anti-bullying Young Person's Advisory Group; the Ethos Committee at Bartholomew School, Eynsham; Joanne-Louise Binns from the Forgotten Children's Foundation; Jo Brown, Lucinda Chambers, Bev Green, Andrew Hamilton and Amanda Page, Melody Evans, Jo Elliott, Zueleka Waheed, and Jon Wood for his patience and IT support.

Special thanks to Maria Huffer, Penny Bassett and Tim Lee (Protective Behaviours UK trainers) for input and guidance on protective behaviours, the concepts and themes of which run through the resource. Protective Behaviours UK has given permission for copyrighted Protective Behaviours content to be included in this resource. Protective behaviours evolved over a number of years, and the ideas and concepts contained in this pack were developed by many people, including Di Margetts.

Many of the exercises in this resource have been reproduced with grateful thanks to Protective Behaviours UK, Penny Bassett and Tim Lee. Maria Huffer contributed to some of the text on Protective Behaviours found in the first part of Section I, 'Working with young people'. Penny Bassett and Tim Lee contributed the text between pages 16 and 22 'Understanding the underlying ideas: Protective Behaviours and Restorative Approaches'. The text between pages 26 and 32 'The young person's experience – understanding the effects of being the victim of a crime', has been adapted with thanks from material written by Victim Support. Exercises that are drawn from Protective Behaviours are 2.1, 2.2, 2.6, 2.10, 3.1, 3.2, 3.7 and 3.8. Exercises 2.3, 2.4 and 3.3 have been adapted from *What Have I Done? A Victim Empathy Programme for Young People* by Pete Wallis with Clair Aldington and Marian Leibmann. Exercise 2.9 was developed by Deborah M Plummer and is from *Helping Children to Build Self-Esteem* and the blob tree exercise is used with the kind permission of Pip Wilson from *Games without Frontiers*. Cover artwork is by Emily Milne Wallis and the majority of the illustrations were kindly produced by Nick Mussell. The images on p.49 were provided by Clair Aldington.

This resource contains case studies. While the issues raised are based on real situations, the names and details have been altered to preserve anonymity. The authors have endeavoured to ensure that the information included is accurate, but the responsibility for any factual errors is our own.

Introduction

What is the purpose of this resource?

The impact of crime on young people and their families can be devastating. This resource has been written to help those supporting the needs of young victims: to help them to understand the experience, to explore its effect upon them including their feelings and reactions, and ultimately to help them to move beyond it.

Research indicates that young people are more likely to be victims of crime than adults and most likely to be victimized by other young people. However, young people are less likely to come forward and report incidents and therefore less able to access support.

In a recent survey, over 35 per cent of young people aged 10 to 15 had experienced at least one personal crime in the previous 12 months. This was about the same level as for those aged 16 to 25 (32%) and well above those aged 26 to 65 (14%) (Wood 2005).

If you are reading this having been approached by a young person who has been the victim of crime and seeking support, you are in a privileged position. *Why Me?* is designed to offer support to you in supporting these young people – the mostly silent majority.

The shock and stigma attached to being a victim of crime often makes it difficult even for adults to report their victimization. For young victims there may be additional obstacles:

- Fear that they will not be believed.
- Fear of being blamed or punished.
- Feelings of guilt, shame and self-blame.
- Fear of retaliation.
- Mistrust of adults.
- Belief that nothing will be done.
- Lack of knowledge about available services.
- Lack of access to services.
- Perceived and real limits of confidentiality.

- Fear of the criminal justice system and of the potential of having to provide evidence in court.

- Lack of understanding that what they experienced was a crime.

These potential obstacles represent a formidable barrier to young people experiencing victimization and may have potentially serious consequences.

Some young people can be extremely resilient, and most cope well in the aftermath of a crime and recover over time even without adult support. They find their own strategies, and often manage to put the experience behind them quite quickly.

Others do less well and some may deteriorate. They may be less able than adults to recover, having not yet developed the coping mechanisms that come with life experience. Many young people are less able to defend themselves, have fewer choices of peers and are more restricted in the places they can go than adults. Those young people more deeply affected, or who fail to recover after a few days, are a particular concern, and the main focus of this resource.

Each person and every situation is unique, and a young person's response to being victimized may not be what you might expect. This resource will encourage you to look at every situation on an individual basis. It is easy to assume that, because an offence is relatively minor in terms of seriousness, the impact on young people will be small. It is the harm experienced by the young people that is important, not our preconceptions – if they are distressed, it matters to them, and we should react accordingly.

There is also a growing recognition of an overlap between offenders and victims, and that some young people may turn to crime in response to becoming victims of crime. These assertions are supported in *The Good Practice Guide for Supporting Young Victims of Crime* (HM Government 2009). So, by supporting victims of crime, you will also be helping to prevent the victimization of other young people in future.

A note on terminology

In general the terms 'victim' and 'offender' are not helpful labels. While they are used occasionally within this resource as the most convenient terms available, We have tried to avoid them where possible, aware that they are potentially damaging labels that should not be used in practice. 'Victim' carries connotations of passivity and even helplessness, while calling someone an 'offender' implies that committing crimes is their only feature. Both terms are best avoided when describing a young person in their presence.

What does this resource comprise?

The resource is divided into three main sections and an accompanying DVD.

Section I: Background explains what the resource is and how it can be used, and provides key suggestions and guidance for those supporting young people. It introduces the principles of 'protective behaviours' and 'restorative approaches', and the basis from which to start work with a young person.

Section II: Exercises and Worksheets details the actual activities to use with young people, with photocopiable handouts and additional notes and tips for the practitioners. It is important to stress that, while they are numbered to help you to make sense of their organization, the exercises and activities included are not designed to be worked through in order or indeed in their entirety. There are too many to use them all, and trying to do so might make a young person feel overwhelmed and bombarded. Just pick the ones you think may be helpful to the particular young people you are working with, taking into account their age, learning style and how defended or open they are in discussing what has happened to them.

Section III: Further Resources provides additional materials that should help you to make the most of the activities – worked case studies based on real examples of how they have been used before – and also expansion activities that accompany the two films featured on the DVD accompanying this resource.

The *Why Me?* DVD has two modules:

1. Module 1 – 'Crime hurts' features young people sharing their real experiences of being victimized.

2. Module 2 – 'Protective behaviours' provides practical insight into how some of the exercises included in this resource may be delivered and incorporated into supportive sessions with young people.

How can this resource be used and by whom?

Why Me? is designed to be used by a practitioner with a young person (though it could be adapted for groupwork) and is intended to be flexible – for the practitioner to be able to pick and choose activities that best meet the needs of the individual. It provides practical exercises and useful tools for anyone in a position to offer their time – be it an hour or ongoing meetings over several months – to give assistance and support to a young person experiencing or at risk of victimization. Although there are no upper or lower age limits to the experiences of crime, the resource has been designed to primarily address the needs of young people aged eight or nine upwards.

The resource is particularly suitable for adults working with young people in any of the following settings: children's homes, children's social care assessment teams, colleges, connexions services, counselling, disability services, faith groups, foster care, leaving care teams, looked after services, health services, mental health services, mediation services, mentoring, police, probation, schools, secure environments, social work, sports coaching, victim support services, witness services and care units, youth justice and youth work. Adults working as volunteers, wardens or with young carers may also find it helpful.

It may be useful too to young people who are peer listeners, peer counsellors, peer mediators, peer mentors or school council members.

The exercises are not specialist or technical and are not intended to be a replacement for more expert or specialist help where it is needed. Key suggestions on recognizing potential signs that a young person has been victimized, and how to assess whether further help may be required, are given in 'The young person's experience – understanding the effects of being the victim of a crime' in Section I.

The exercises are rooted in two underlying ideas – 'protective behaviours' and 'restorative approaches', principles which are explained in more detail in Section I. The activities are intended to focus on safety, offer helpful decision-making strategies and provide a simple and effective framework for addressing harm.

Why Me? is written to be read and used on its own, but those who wish to seek out more background knowledge may be interested in its 'sister' publication, *Are You Okay? A Practical Guide to Helping Young Victims of Crime* by Pete Wallis, which is a handy guide for practitioners providing information and advice for anyone approached by a young person who has become the victim of a criminal offence, or anyone who is likely to encounter a young person who has been victimized.

Section I:
Background

Working with young people
Starting out

Before you carry out any of the exercises in this resource, we recommend that you familiarize yourself with its overall content, as detailed in the introduction. Once you are familiar with the potential of the resource, the starting point for the use of any of the exercises is to focus on the experiences of the young people themselves.

If they feel victimized, their experience is valid whether or not it is reported as a crime, whether or not they are injured and whether or not it falls under the usual offence categories. This resource has been designed to assist young people in exploring what they are feeling in creative and useful ways that are aimed to lead to real insight and resolution.

Many young people who have experienced victimization struggle to clearly identify and speak about what they are feeling and experiencing, but they can show or enact, draw or play out their feelings and thoughts well. However they need to be given the right 'tools' to do this. For some this may be writing; for others, drawing; for others it might be through play or role play. Therefore many of the exercises within this resource offer alternative, creative, imaginative and playful exploratory tools to address harm and increase feelings of safety.

Whether this is your first time working with a young person, or whether you have considerable experience in this type of work, this stage is an important starting point. Considering your approach to the work before you meet the young person will help promote good practice and contribute to a successful outcome. You may find that some of the ideas that feature are within new territory; others may build on your present working methods. We invite you to have a go at trying out an idea or suggestion even if it is perhaps something different for you.

Understanding the underlying ideas – Protective Behaviours and Restorative Approaches
Protective Behaviours

'Protective behaviours' is a practical and down-to-earth approach to personal safety made up of two themes and seven supporting strategies. It originated in the 1970s in response to an observation that many young people lacked the skills to protect themselves from abuse – physical, sexual or emotional – and so were suffering in silence for long periods before asking for help. Although initially an abuse prevention strategy, it has evolved to be used in a wide range of settings and by a variety of people and organizations. In addition to abuse prevention, it has been used in bullying prevention, crime prevention, crisis intervention, counselling, mentoring, assertiveness training, staff development, parent support work, mediation and conflict resolution, to name a few.

The protective behaviours process: It has been said that the greatest truths are the simplest and the protective behaviours process is based on two very simple truths or, as they are called, two themes:

- Theme 1 – we all have the right to feel safe all the time.

- Theme 2 – there is nothing so awful or small that we can't talk about it with someone.

Supporting the two themes are the seven protective behaviours strategies:

- Protective interruption.

- Persistence.

- One step removed.

- Risking for a purpose.

- Theme reinforcement.

- Network review.

- The language of safety.

Theme 1 – we all have the right to feel safe all the time: Fundamental to the protective behaviours process is the affirmation of the right to feel safe. Encouraging people to believe that they have this right will give them the confidence to seek help when they feel unsafe. How do we know when we are not feeling safe? By tuning into our 'early warning signs', those messages our body gives (butterflies in the stomach, wobbly knees, pounding heart, etc.) that let us know that something is not right in a particular situation. These early warning signs are our gut feelings – our intuition, our subconscious mind communicating with our conscious mind. We have no choice or control over them. But we can choose how to respond.

Theme 1 highlights the links between rights and responsibilities. It also takes the concepts of blame and punishment out of commonly held ideas associated with responsibilities. Instead the 'ability to respond' contained within the meaning of the word is emphasized.

Safety is viewed on a continuum:

- Feeling safe.

- Fun to feel scared (where we choose to feel unsafe because the scary feelings are the goal (e.g. fairground rides)).

- Risking for a purpose (definitely not fun but a means to a goal (e.g. sitting exams, having surgery)).

- Feeling unsafe.

This final situation is considered a personal emergency, because individuals are in danger of losing control over what happens to them. This is where Theme 2 of protective behaviours comes in.

Theme 2 – there is nothing so awful or small that we can't talk about it with someone: Theme 2 encourages the development of a clear support network that you can call upon when you have identified that you are feeling unsafe. Members of a network should be accessible, reliable, able to listen and able to take action with you but not necessarily for you. Having several people on a network should mean that there is always one person available and suitable to discuss any concern that you may have. Talking with members of a network can provide guidance, reduce stress, open up new opportunities and so improve our ability to make choices that are in our best interests.

The seven strategies: Linked to the two protective behaviour themes are seven supporting strategies. These serve two main purposes – to reinforce the effectiveness of the two themes and to provide additional guidance on how to respond when you feel vulnerable or unsafe.

- Protective interruption – any action we take to interrupt or halt any potential or actual unsafe situation – for instance, saying 'no' when someone is trying to do something we feel is wrong.

- Persistence – persisting in seeking help until we feel safe again and our early warning signs have gone. This includes seeking further help if our early warning signs return. Persistence is also important in long-term personal commitments – for example, studying for exams, learning a new skill, tackling addiction. Don't give up at the first hurdle!

- One step removed – using a 'third person', indirect approach to problem solving, to seek assistance or to check out someone's ideas before making a disclosure. Taking a step back and looking at the situation from different angles, to encourage creative, lateral thinking to open up new ideas. For a worker assisting a young person in role play, the use of videos or puppets would be a one step removed approach.

- Risking for a purpose – deliberately choosing to take a risk, even though we may not feel safe, because we have a longer term goal (e.g. disclosing that one has been the victim of a crime).

- Theme reinforcement – reinforcing the two themes verbally, visually and especially by example.

- Network review – people and situations change so we regularly need to check that our networks are available, helpful and still suited to our needs.

- The language of safety – this is the glue that holds all the protective behaviour elements together. It includes re-framing our language into an empowering, non-victimizing and non-violent format that is consistent with the protective behaviours process. This approach acknowledges that language is a powerful tool in forming and maintaining a positive self-image. It also demonstrates the difference between 'political correctness' when we do not need to believe in what we are saying, and protective behaviours language where the guiding principle is whether someone is likely to feel unsafe because of our choice of words.

Additional protective behaviours concepts: In addition to the two themes and seven strategies, protective behaviours highlight a number of other important concepts – in particular, the unwritten rules of society and the interaction of feelings, thoughts and behaviour.

Unwritten rules of society: In every aspect of life there are rules that affect our behaviour. Many are written down – the *Highway Code*, the law, health and safety regulations. There are also many rules that influence our behaviour but they are not written down. They are expectations other people put on us, and we put on ourselves. They act as a guide to social interaction and many of them can be very helpful, but sometimes not. These are what we call the 'unwritten rules of society'. We may not believe them, or agree with them, but they can still affect our behaviour. For example, men should be good at DIY, women should look after the children, boys don't cry, girls wear pink.

The relevance of unwritten rules of society for protective behaviours is as follows:

- They can on occasions be unhelpful because they hold us back when we need to take action to protect our own safety (e.g. not to report an incident to the police).

- If we don't follow the unwritten rules of society (e.g. having the right clothing and image), we may feel inadequate and we may be ostracized or bullied.

- They can hold us back from achieving our full potential or getting the most out of life (e.g. boys don't do ballet).

It is therefore important for us to recognize when an unhelpful unwritten rule is operating so that we can have the confidence to challenge it and take action to ensure our own safety.

Feelings, thoughts and behaviour: Protective behaviours explore the interaction between our feelings, thoughts and behaviour. We believe that feelings are feelings, neither right nor wrong, good nor bad. Getting in touch with our feelings helps free our mind for thinking. Our thinking can influence both our feelings and behaviour.

By separating feelings, thoughts and behaviour, we are able to make informed decisions about how to respond. The goal is to tune into our feelings, and think about options – there are always more than we think at first. We include all options, not just the good ones, as we look at the effects of each option and then choose what to do, which option is the best at this point in time.

Feelings are feelings; behaviour is a choice, always with an effect – our thinking influences both.

Practical explanations of how the themes and strategies can be introduced for your support of young people are provided throughout Section I. Exercises and activities based on particular protective behaviour concepts are contained within Section II of this resource.

Restorative Approaches

Restorative justice works hand in hand with protective behaviours, and is based upon core values and principles that will be central in your work with young people, whether or not they get to meet the person who hurt them. All your engagement will be voluntary, and based upon honesty, trust and respect. A restorative approach avoids judging people, and accepts that those with a problem are usually best placed to find their own solution. As a supportive adult, it is important to maintain an open attitude of empathic listening to help them explore their options, while avoiding offering unsolicited advice.

If you model and embody these values and principles, which are summarized here, the young people will feel safe and supported, and empowered to take steps to reclaim their lives, which might include courageously asking to meet the very person who hurt them.

Key restorative principles and values include:

- respectful relationships

- a belief in everyone's ability to find their own solutions

- a focus on minimizing harm and damage to people

- honesty and openness

- trust and integrity

- tolerance

- taking responsibility

- collaboration

- active listening, sensitive checking and exploration of meanings

- an open and non-judgemental approach

- a commitment to empowering and developing confidence in others

- valuing others, inclusion and acceptance of diversity

- care with the ownership of information.

In some cases, the young people you are supporting won't know who hurt them, and the perpetrator may never be apprehended. However, most crimes against young people are committed by other young people, and, because the perpetrator is likely to be a peer, the young people you are supporting may know exactly whom it was who hurt them. The incident may have been a one-off, but it may be part of an ongoing conflict. Some young people see their attacker every day – for example, in class or in their street. There may be unresolved questions and issues – most commonly, 'Why did this happen?', 'Why was I targeted?' and 'Will it happen again?'

A restorative approach, involving carefully supported communication between the two parties, can be a helpful way to move things forward. In the context of your support for young people, they may have developed good strategies for keeping safe, and now have the confidence to take a risk for a purpose. They may express a desire to sort out the conflict that led to their being hurt. A restorative process helps them to regain control, tell their story and receive answers to those most pressing questions – from the only person who knows.

Restorative enquiry

At the heart of the restorative approach is the restorative enquiry, which is a helpful framework for exploring a crime or incident with a young person. Skilful questioning helps you and the young person understand their anxieties, emotions and assumptions. It indicates that you want to hear their concerns. The key questions are:

- 'What has happened?'

- 'What were you thinking at the time?'

- 'How were you feeling at the time?'

- 'What do you think about it now?'

- 'How are you feeling now?'

- 'Who else has been affected by what happened?'

- 'What do you need now to feel better?'

- 'What needs to happen for the harm to be repaired?'

You may want to explore the whole incident, from the events leading up to it, to the actual incident, what happened straight afterwards and what has happened since. These same questions can be used at significant points in their story, but avoid asking too many. Avoid slipping into interrogation mode. The restorative enquiry can be used for either party in a conflict. If they are struggling to speak clearly and fully, they can show, enact, draw or play their feelings about it. They can tick boxes for questions or show you on a feelings chart or with feelings cards (see Resources).

Many schools, police services, youth offending services, care homes and other agencies are developing services for restorative justice. Although this is a common-sense approach and you will have many of the skills already, bringing parties together in a meeting to resolve a conflict is sensitive work. You can use this resource without formal restorative justice training, but, if you have had such training, you might also consider facilitating a meeting between the two parties.

If you have not undertaken formal training (which typically lasts four to five days), find out if there is a service that could facilitate a meeting for your young person and the perpetrator of the crime. If the perpetrator is an adult, there may be a restorative justice service within the probation service or police. Remember that the communication doesn't always have to involve a face-to-face meeting – an exchange of messages, letters, gifts, etc. can also be powerful. Also, it is often helpful to involve the families, who are likely to have been affected by the incident.

Establishing a safe place for your work

Before deciding the best location for your sessions, you may want to consider discussing this with the young people you're going to be working with. It might be harder to engage them if they have not been part of the decision-making process. It is often assumed that the place they will feel most comfortable and safe in is their own home. This may not, however, be possible for some supporters for example, teachers and youth workers. When arranging a place to work, you could consider contacting the young people to talk with them about the best place for you both. This is an ideal opportunity to make first contact in a safe way and, by offering them the choice, it gives them some control over what happens next.

During your work together you are likely to be discussing emotive and personally challenging issues. Sessions will be more productive if you and the young person feel safe and comfortable in the work space and there won't be disruptions from other people. The young person will have to open up and focus on internal experiences at times, which is unlikely to happen in a threatening or distracting environment. The first key theme of the protective behaviour process is the belief that everyone has the right to feel safe all the time. This includes you and the young person you are working with. It is about feeling safe as opposed to being safe.

Your place of work is likely to have clear guidance on lone working arrangements and it is always advisable to plan the action you might want to take if, on arrival at your agreed venue or meeting place, your intuitive feelings or 'early warning signs' are telling you that you do not feel safe. The same consideration applies to the young person too. Early warning signs are the physical body responses that tell us when we do not feel safe (e.g. butterflies in the stomach, pounding heart, shaky legs) and we need to do something about it. When meeting young people, you could ask them if the venue feels safe and comfortable for them too.

Creating a supportive working environment
Working agreements
Although this resource is designed to be used in an informal setting, without boundary-keeping and working agreements or ground rules in place, there may be confusion and the learning experience could be less effective. Both you and the young person will work more effectively if these 'unwritten rules' are clear, realistic, empowering and safe. If they are discussed as part of your first session, you will both have a shared understanding of session expectations. For example, the unwritten rules may be to inform each other if you are not going to be able to attend a scheduled meeting, to listen to each other, to be non-judgemental.

Confidentiality
The first session is usually the time when confidentiality is discussed. In preparation for this, you may want to check that you know your organization's policies and procedures on child protection issues. As your working relationship evolves with the young people, they may feel safe enough to disclose to you. They need to be clear about your confidentiality policy and what actions follow such disclosure.

Explaining this in a supportive way without creating a communication barrier can be difficult. We suggest talking with young people about their right to feel safe and that, if they mention something that has been a violation of that right, then, to support them, you may have to talk with someone else about it to get the help they need. You can also say that, if they tell you something and you are aware of personal early warning signs, you know you need to talk with someone on your network; this is likely to be a designated person as part of your child protection policy. Your instinct and intuitive feelings may tell you that the time the young people have chosen to disclose is not the safest for them. You will need to 'protectively interrupt' to prevent the disclosure, but offer a time when they are less vulnerable. Any action we take to interrupt or halt any potential or actual unsafe situation, can be referred to as 'protective interruption'.

Introducing these ideas in this context is modelling some of the strategies you will be discussing in later sessions.

Good communication

Throughout your relationship with the young people you are supporting, including when working with them through some of the exercises and activities, there is an important emphasis on communication.

As detailed earlier, the second key theme of the protective behaviour process is that there is nothing so awful or so small that we can't talk about it with someone. We can use someone on our personal network to get support. We talk to them to get the response we need. Good communication skills, including the language you use, provide consistency with the content of any materials and resources chosen. The importance of language as 'the glue' that holds all the ideas together is essential when using the exercises in this resource with young people.

The way we communicate includes both verbal and non-verbal messages as well as body language. The following points will help you in your sessions:

- The language of safety – use a language that observes everyone's right to feel safe. This is based on our internal response, not the unwritten rules associated with being 'politically correct'.

- Quality of language – use invitational language as opposed to being authoritative. Suggest that a young person may want to complete an exercise, rather than giving an instruction. Use empowering phrases and language that build confidence and self-esteem. Consider challenging abusive, racist, violent, sexist or any language that denigrates someone.

- Shared meaning – ensure that you and the young person you are working with understand what each of you is saying. Do your words mean the same thing, particularly when it comes to using 'street' language? Acronyms you use may mean nothing to the young person.

- Clarity – be clear about what it is you are trying to say. This seems obvious, but sometimes we assume people know what we mean or that the same unwritten rules apply without our saying it again. This can lead to confusion.

- Ownership – this is about taking responsibility for our language, our feelings, thoughts and behaviour. Encourage the use of 'I feel...' as opposed to 'You make me feel...'; 'How do you feel when...?' as opposed to 'How does that make you feel?'; 'What did you think when…?' as opposed to 'What did that make you think?'; 'I did this because…' as opposed to 'They made me do this.'

- Unwritten rules – one easy way to recognize when an unwritten rule is coming into play is when we use or hear the words 'should', 'ought' and 'must'. This can be imposing a feeling, thought or action on to someone else, and it is not invitational. Encourage the questioning of such commands by saying, 'Do I need to do this, or will this affect my ability to keep myself feeling safe?'

- Encourage a 'talking with' approach – talking with someone creates a dialogue. You could discuss with the young people the qualities they would look for in someone they would want on their personal network. This might include an exploration of what good listening skills are and how they feel they want to be treated – that is; with respect, without being judged unfairly, be believed.

- Using one step removed – this ensures that you and the young person can keep feeling safe by using a 'third person' approach for addressing challenging, sensitive or emotive issues. It provides you with a safe way into discussing specific feelings, thoughts and behaviours. You could say, for example, 'How might someone feel when…?', or 'When might someone feel sad/scared/fearful…?' or 'How might someone react/ behave/respond to…?'

Attitudes and beliefs

Before starting this type of work with a young person, it can be useful to reflect on your own attitudes and beliefs (unwritten rules) about crime, people who commit crimes and those who are affected by it. These may shape how you carry out this work and respond to the needs of the young person. We suggest caution when labelling someone, for example, as a victim, perpetrator or bully.

Problem solving

The work you are undertaking can be challenging and we suggest using some of the strategies in this resource for yourself to ensure that you feel safe and can solve difficult situations. Use your feelings as a guide and think about the different options you have before making a decision about any action you may take. Remember to use your own personal network of support and consider arranging supervision sessions as part of your overall plan for this work. The resource encourages young people to use strategies to problem solve for themselves; your responsibility is to facilitate this and not to solve every problem for them. It is your responsibility to take care of your own emotional needs.

Educational experience

You might find it helpful to find out about the young person's educational history, academic ability and whether they have any specific learning requirements. The resource contains a range of techniques and approaches, but you may need to think about how accessible some of the activities are for the young person and any adaptations that may need to be made.

Reviewing

Whether the contact you have with the young people you are working with is a one-off informal brief meeting or ongoing sessions over a number of weeks, it is good practice to review with them after each meeting, or at the beginning of the next, what has been discussed. This provides an opportunity to ensure that both you and they have 'shared meaning' – that is, understand what each is saying. This is also a good opportunity to identify any progress made or to agree next steps. Next steps may be to agree to refer a young person on for additional support. Or it may be that a young person chooses to end their contact with you. Be prepared for this. Consider who will be most affected if the young person does choose to opt out. If your early warning signs indicate that informing others of young people's decisions supports their right to feel safe, explain and discuss this with the young people in a supportive way and share with them the suggested next steps.

The young person's experience – understanding the effects of being a victim of a crime

We now detail some common effects experienced by young people who are victimized. It is worth retaining an awareness of these symptoms when working with young people and, where appropriate, taking care to make a referral to the relevant authorities when one is required (e.g. in the case of post-traumatic stress).

PHYSIOLOGICAL EFFECTS

Young people are likely to experience a number of physical reactions that occur prior to, during or after their experience of crime or victimization or when the memory of the crime returns.

Immediately before (also known as early warning signs), or at the time:

- increased heart rate

- shaking

- tears

- numbness

- a feeling of being frozen or experiencing events in slow motion

- a dryness of the mouth or being sick

- loss of bowel or bladder control

- heightened sensory perception (e.g. smell or hearing).

After the incident:

- inability to sleep

- changes in appetite

- lethargy

- headaches

- muscle tension

- nausea.

These reactions and others may persist for some time after the event occurred. In addition a young person may be physically hurt during the crime, such as in an assault. Common injuries include those to the head and face, broken facial bones (nose, cheekbone, lower jaw etc.), hand injuries, bruising to upper limbs (warding off punches etc.) and broken or missing teeth. Over time, some physical injuries will heal but others will not and may leave a permanent reminder of the crime (adapted from Victim Support 2009).

PSYCHOLOGICAL EFFECTS

Crime or victimization can have a greater psychological effect on young people than natural or man-made disasters because people who commit a crime have done so with the intention to cause harm. The psychological consequences can continue for a long time after an event.

Emotions and feelings after a crime can include the following:

- anxiety and fear

- anger

- shock

- disbelief

- distress

- grief

- a feeling of helplessness.

It is quite normal for young people who have suffered crime or victimization to experience some or all of these emotions very strongly after a crime. They may shake with fear, and can be easily startled. They may express anger towards the perpetrator, bystanders, society, the police, friends, family or themselves. They may seem to be numb and 'brush off' the impact of the crime. They may cry and sob. The intensity and the lack of control that young people may feel they have over these feelings can seem quite overwhelming.

Many young people blame themselves for what has happened. They may believe that the crime was 'their fault' because they left their property on view or provoked violence. To some extent, guilt represents an effort to understand the event and to restructure it so that it cannot happen again. If the young person comes to believe that their behaviour provoked the assault, it puts them back in control, because they can alter their behaviour to prevent the crime from happening again.

Being victimized can increase a young person's fear of becoming a victim again – a very logical response, because repeat victimization can be common. They may fear that the same person or someone else will repeat the offence against them and that next time the crime or the consequences will be more serious.

A young person who suffered an aggravated burglary said:

> I was very alert after, more alert than previously… This thing still lingered on my mind that somebody could break in and attack me in bed… It's made me think that this thing could happen to me again, or it could happen to anyone.

A young person who was assaulted said:

> I'm really wary… It's a general fear… A small bunch of people roaming the streets late at night… To me that's lethal now… They might actually kill.

The assumption that the world is a predictable and fair place, and that others are trustworthy, can be shattered as a result of crime.

Other people can be blamed for the crime. These may include the perpetrator, bystanders, the police or society at large. On occasion young people who experience crime may blame particular groups (e.g. black people, young people or men). This may have a negative effect on their future relationships with individuals from these groups. Being a victim of crime can also affect people's religious beliefs.

Equally it is not uncommon for young people who are victimized to view positively what others would see as a wholly negative experience. This can be understood as a natural way of reinterpreting the experience to fit in with their existing belief systems. For example, one young person who was beaten around the head said, 'I was lucky I was wearing glasses. If I'd have been wearing contact lenses, I'd probably have lost my sight.' Young victims may even express concern for the person who hurt them. For example, they may feel sympathy for the desperate state that they must have been in to commit such a crime.

Flashbacks are memories of the experience relived. They are more that just a memory and can also involve physical reactions such as increased heart rate. Trigger events and flashbacks can lead the young person to experience the emotional effects of the crime as strongly as before. Flashbacks can be quite common following a crime, but in most cases they decline markedly in the weeks following the assault.

BEHAVIOURAL EFFECTS

Crime is likely to have some effect on a young person's behaviour. This may occur immediately after the event or some time later. The effect on their behaviour can include the following:

The young person will commonly avoid people and places that they associate with crime. Examples include:

- their houses (if the crime occurred in or near to their house, a young person may move house)

- avoiding areas, situations or people that remind them of the crime

- withdrawing from social contact

- attempting to alter their behaviour or appearance.

Young people sometimes use alcohol and drugs as a coping mechanism and to relieve emotional pain. Some say that experiencing violent crime improves their relationships while others can become withdrawn. If a young person changes their view of the world as a result of crime, this can also affect their relationships. For example, they may blame partners or friends for failing to protect them, or they may become distrustful of other people so they are less likely to develop friendships.

POST-TRAUMATIC STRESS DISORDER

Post-traumatic stress disorder (PTSD) is a psychological and physical condition that is caused by very frightening or distressing events. It occurs in up to 30 per cent of people who experience traumatic events.

PTSD requires appropriate intervention and can be successfully treated. For more information look at the NHS website in the non-book resources section. Potential symptoms include:

- Flashbacks – sudden and vivid reliving of the incident, including nightmares, although they can occur at any time. They can involve physical reactions such as increased heart rate.

- Triggers – where something or someone will remind victims of an aspect of the initial experience, and lead to feelings of distress similar to those they felt at the time, which may be debilitating (e.g. fireworks triggering a startle response).

- Panic attacks – due to the release of hormones such as adrenalin, characteristic of the 'fight or flight' response (not related to events in the 'here and now') where a situation, (perhaps as a reminder of the crime or abuse) causes sweating, chest pains, difficulty in breathing, hyperventilation, high blood pressure, numbness, fainting, dizziness or tingling in the extremities.

- Hyper-alertness – where the body keeps producing the stress hormone cortisol telling the brain there is a threat, even when there isn't. This leaves the person tense, on guard and agitated, with no inner peace, as if the incident is recurring. An innocent pat on the shoulder may lead to a violent and inappropriate reaction.

- Avoidance – efforts to avoid thoughts, feelings, activities, situations or people likely to remind the person of the traumatic experience.

- Obsessive-compulsive rituals – as an attempt by people to organize and control their external world, when they have little or no control over their inner world.

- Self-harming – as a control strategy to regulate inner emotional turmoil.

PTSD is particularly linked with experiences that involve loss of control, being unable to stop a bad experience from happening, fear of serious injury or death, and not knowing when the experience will end – some or all of which may be associated with a crime.

People suffering PTSD may feel insecure and suffer low self-esteem. They may lose the ability to make new relationships or maintain existing relationships with family, friends and partners.

Some suggestions for dealing with PTSD are as follows:

- If some of these symptoms are present or your intuition tells you something isn't right, seek a formal diagnosis by a qualified medical practitioner.

- A health practitioner such as a physiotherapist may be able to help with relaxation and advice on reversing the body's stress response with breathing exercises, posture and gentle movements.

- Yoga and mindfulness meditation can be helpful.

- Some of these services may be available via a GP, or accessed privately. Information can be found via the internet although personal recommendation from friends or family can be useful.

TAKING CARE WHEN OBSERVING SYMPTOMS

While it may seem useful to use this discussion as a way to categorize the response of the individuals you encounter, each person's experience is unique, and young people react in different ways to a crime. The psychological effects of crime may lead to physical effects. For example, fear and anxiety may be expressed in restlessness, feeling shaky, shortness of breath, accelerated heart rate, nausea, difficulty concentrating, difficulty in falling or staying asleep. Essentially, everyone will experience an incident differently and recover from crime at different rates and speeds. Factors that may affect recovery include:

- the severity of the crime

- prior mental health issues

- age

- gender

- the nature of the attack

- the victim's relationship with the perpetrator

- previous experience of being a victim

- coping abilities

- networks of social support

- support from professional helpers

- reporting to the police

- how other people respond to the victim.

Bullying

Because bullying is a substantial problem and something that many young people will experience, we now include some more detail about the nature of bullying. Bullying can occur in many different forms:

- Calling someone names.

- Spreading rumours or gossip about someone.

- Threatening someone to their face or by text or email.

- Hitting, kicking, punching, spitting or tripping someone up.

- Stealing someone's things like lunch money or clothes.

- Throwing someone's possessions around.

- Ruining someone's property or work.

- Ignoring someone or leaving them out of a group.

- Peer pressure or manipulation.

- Intimidating or threatening someone using gestures.

- Making fun of someone or singling them out for being different (that is, because of their skin colour, perceived sexuality, religion, disability or perhaps even because they are clever).

- Putting someone under pressure to act or look in a certain way.

- Making someone do something that they don't want to do, or stopping them from doing something that they do want to do.

- Forcing someone to pick on someone else to appear tough or be accepted as part of a group.

- Writing offensive graffiti about someone.

- Forcing someone to act in a sexual manner or touching them when they don't want you to.

- Prank calling.

- Setting up a hate site or group or posting abusive messages on social networking sites.

Not all the things listed here are against the law or a crime, but they can be very hurtful and bullying can form a part in all crimes. The starting point for supporting young people is their experience of what has happened to them. If they feel victimized, their experience is valid whether or not it is reported as a crime, whether or not they are injured, and whether or not it falls under the usual offence categories.

Remember, if you have been approached by young people who have experienced crime or victimization and are seeking support, you are in a privileged position. We hope that you will find this resource useful as you help to support them – there is no set prescription of tools to aid young people in their recovery, just as there are no standard incidents experienced by all young victims, but we hope that you will find the exercises that follow a rich source of ideas.

Section II:
Exercises and Worksheets

Module 1:
Getting to know me and what's happened

1.1 Getting to know me

This exercise provides young people with an opportunity to say what they think about themselves and their situation. It can be used to enhance your working relationship with them and, while it is not to be used as a formal assessment tool, it can support the identification of areas for further exploration. In addition, it can highlight areas of particular concern that may require a more urgent response.

Instructions

Ask the young person:

> On a scale of 0 to 5 with 0 meaning that you strongly disagree with the statement and 5 meaning that you strongly agree, circle the number that best represents where you see yourself right now.

Tips

- Use when you feel an ice-breaker would be useful.

- Use answers as discussion starters.

- Use on your first and last session with a young person to review change.

GETTING TO KNOW ME

0 = strongly disagree; 5 = strongly agree

I feel good about myself	0 1 2 3 4 5
I like where I live	0 1 2 3 4 5
I feel safe at home	0 1 2 3 4 5
I feel safe at school	0 1 2 3 4 5
I feel safe when I'm out and about	0 1 2 3 4 5
I know who to go to or phone if I need help	0 1 2 3 4 5
I feel loved and cared for	0 1 2 3 4 5
I generally trust other people	0 1 2 3 4 5
I treat people with respect	0 1 2 3 4 5
I like playing or spending time with my friends	0 1 2 3 4 5
I sleep well at night	0 1 2 3 4 5
I have people I can talk to if I am worried	0 1 2 3 4 5
I have lots of strengths	0 1 2 3 4 5
I have choices about what to do in life	0 1 2 3 4 5
I feel positive about my future	0 1 2 3 4 5
I belong to a club or group outside school	0 1 2 3 4 5

Thanks for helping us get to know you!

Name .... Date ....

1.2 My shield

This exercise can be used as an alternative, creative ice-breaker. It can assist young people to express who they are and what's important to them.

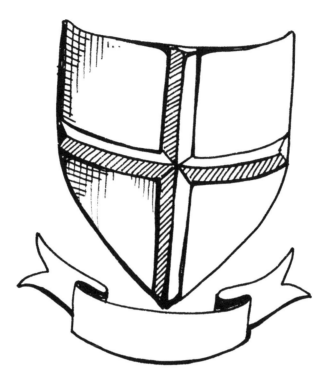

Instructions

Suggest the young people draw the outline of a shield on a flip-chart or large piece of paper if available, including a scroll underneath.

In each of the four segments, suggest that they draw or write something that is important to them, that they like or are good at. It might be that they like socializing with friends, listening to music or walking the dog.

In the scroll underneath, ask them to write something, either a word or a saying that describes them or is their motto.

Tips

- This can also be used as an exercise to build confidence or self-esteem by asking the young people to fill the segments with drawings of things that they are good at or that they have achieved in their lives.

- It can be useful too in helping young people think about how they would like to be.

MY SHIELD

In each of the segments draw or write something. It could be something important to you, or that you like or are good at. In the scroll underneath, write something. It could be either a word or a saying that describes you or is your motto.

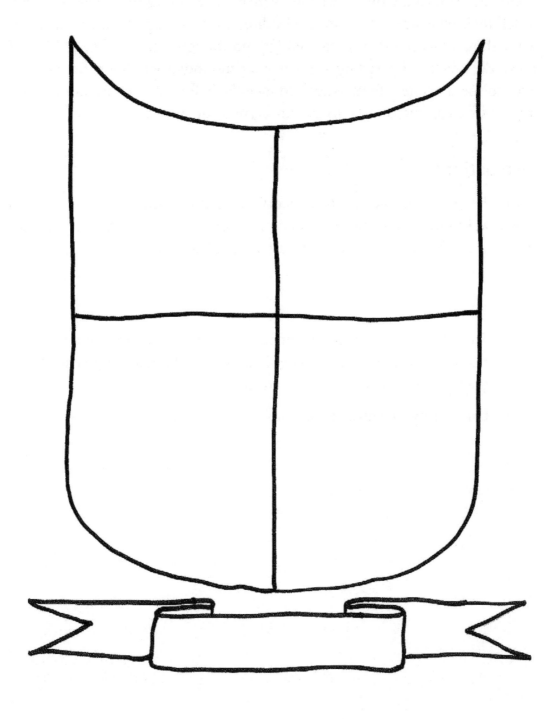

Name . . . . Date . . . .

1.3 Telling it like it was...

This exercise helps enable young people to tell their story of what has happened to them, and for their feelings, thoughts and actions before, during and after the incident to be explored. By telling their story, new possibilities for acceptance, movement and change may open up which can be transformative. By revisiting what happened with the young people, we can look for signs of change, helping them to see the experience in a new light.

The diagram is a timeline, leading from before the incident to the incident itself, and then to the time after the incident. The young people are encouraged to tell their own story of the events leading up to, during and after the incident. They should identify their own feelings and thoughts at each key point up and down the timeline, by writing in the feeling and thought bubbles. Be prepared to expand the timeline – for example, to include 'before' as well as 'just before', or 'now' as well as 'just after' – to capture significant events.

Instructions

Invite the young people to tell the story of what happened to them. They may like to write down in the feeling and thought bubbles what they were feeling and thinking just before, during and just after what happened.

Tips

- To make the exercise more dynamic, use flip-chart paper or a white board, with ready-made thought and feeling bubbles to give to the young person to write on and attach.

- Use writing, pictures or cartoons.

TELLING IT LIKE IT WAS...

Tell the story of what happened to you. You may like to write down in the feeling and thought bubbles what you were feeling and thinking just before, during and just after what happened.

My feelings   What happened   My thoughts

Just before

During

Just after

Name . . . . Date . . . .

Module 2:
Exploring feelings, thoughts and behaviour

2.1 Early warning signs

This exercise helps young people identify the physical signs that occur when they don't feel safe. It can be a starting point for exploring strategies to action when early warning signs are felt.

Instructions

Draw a large outline of a person or use the template on the following page. Ask the young people to think about what happens in their body when they don't feel safe. Try to help them come up with their own ideas, but it may help to give some examples such as butterflies in the stomach, pounding heart or shaky legs.

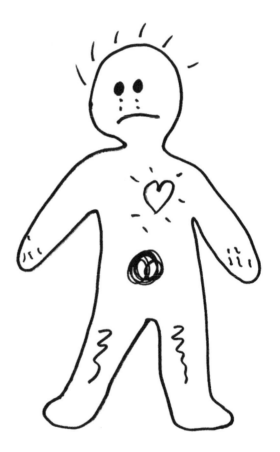

Tips

- Be as creative as you can!

- You could draw around the young people on lining paper and ask them to add their signs using different colours and shapes.

EARLY WARNING SIGNS

What happens in our bodies when we don't feel safe?

    We call these body signs our **early warnings signs**.

    You can draw or write your own early warning signs in the picture below.

Name . . . . Date . . . .

2.2 Feelings, thoughts and behaviour

This exercise can be a decision-making tool. It helps young people to look at the interaction between feelings, thoughts and behaviour. The starting point for this exercise is the young people's experience and their feelings associated with what has happened to them. Being in touch with feelings helps to free up thinking. Thinking can influence both feelings and behaviour. Behaviour is a choice with effects that usually involve others as well as ourselves.

Feelings aren't good or bad, right or wrong. They are our body's way of telling us something. However, how we choose to respond could be good or bad, right or wrong.

Instructions

Use the 'Feelings, Thoughts and Behaviour' template or suggest to the young person that they might like to draw their own. In the 'What happened?' section suggest that they write some words or draw some pictures to describe what happened to them (e.g. 'I was bullied on the way home from school'). The young person can use the 'Feelings' column to write or draw the feelings that they have experienced following the event. Suggest that they use the 'What do I think?' column to write or draw the thoughts that they have had following the event. Encourage the young person to consider the choices that they have and to write or draw them in the 'What choices do I have?' column. For each of the choices identified by the young person, suggest that they consider the possible effects that each choice may have for themselves and others (i.e. their family, friends, boyfriend, girlfriend). Suggest to them that they write or draw their answers in the 'Possible effects' column. Encourage the young person to consider all of the things they have identified. In the final section, 'Behaviour: What do I choose to do? What will keep me and others safe?', suggest that they write or draw the behaviour that they are going to choose to take following what has happened to them.

Tips

- To be able to explain this exercise it is important to try it yourself with a real situation that you are addressing.

- Remember that some people mask one feeling with another, or use behaviour as a way of avoiding or hiding feelings.

- Use the prompt suggestions on pp.45–46 to help the young person.

Prompt suggestions

What is the situation, issue or problem? Ask the young person to consider these questions when completing the exercise on p.47.

FEELINGS

- Write down all my feelings – remember that they are neither good nor bad, right nor wrong. It's what I do with my feelings that could be good or bad.

- What feelings am I showing?

- What feelings am I keeping to myself?

- How is my body affected?

THOUGHTS

- What am I thinking? What are the facts of the situation?

- What are my beliefs and opinions about the situation?

- Have I observed, gathered and remembered all the facts?

- Have I clearly expressed my feelings and thoughts – am I being honest with myself and others?

- Write down all thoughts – get them out, acknowledge them.

OPTIONS

- What do I want to happen? Be creative. Don't worry about how appropriate the ideas might seem at this stage.

- The longer the list and greater the flexibility, the more likely I'll make a good choice at the right time.

- Have I consulted others about the possible options?

- What might others want to happen?

POSSIBLE EFFECTS

- Look ahead to the possible effects. This is a skill that can be improved with experience, so please keep practising.

- What might happen as a result of each of the different options?

- Are the effects safe and respectful to me as well as others?

BEHAVIOUR

- I may need to compromise in order to remedy conflict.

- I may need to plan, prepare and practise.

- In order to implement a decision, full account should be taken of personal strengths and available support. Although I need to make decisions *for* myself, I do not need to make them *by* myself.

- Choose the best solution – take action.

- If there are no safe solutions, revisit the 'Feelings' column and start the process again – maybe something was missed.

Reflect – after the event look back. This will help in future situations.

FEELINGS, THOUGHTS AND BEHAVIOUR

Event – what happened?			
Feelings	**Thoughts**		
How do I feel?	What do I think?	What choices do I have?	Possible effects of these choices?
Behaviour			
What do I choose to do?		What will keep me and others safe?	

Name . . . . Date . . . .

2.3 My feelings graph

A feelings graph encourages a wider vocabulary of feelings, and is a way of illustrating how feelings and emotions change over a period of time.

Instructions

On a sheet of paper draw a graph with feelings on the vertical axis (from 0 representing 'very sad' at the bottom to 10 for 'very happy' at the top) and time on the horizontal axis from morning to night time.

Ask the young person to draw a feelings graph for the day on which the incident happened (or for one of the incidents if there were several). The graph can be adapted to cover the week of the incident if significant events would otherwise be missed.

Tips

- If the young people need to practise the technique, you could ask them to choose any day to do a feelings graph, as a lead-in to this exercise.

- You may like to have a supply of art resources available, including coloured paper, stickers of smiley and sad faces, crayons, etc., to help a young person engage in the exercise.

- A feelings graph can be drawn in the same way, for a young person's life from birth to the present day.

- Encourage the young person to reflect on the highs and lows of their experience, their strengths, coping strategies, support networks and the fact that they have survived.

MY FEELINGS GRAPH

Draw a feelings graph for the day that the incident happened to you. Try to remember key moments when your feelings changed.

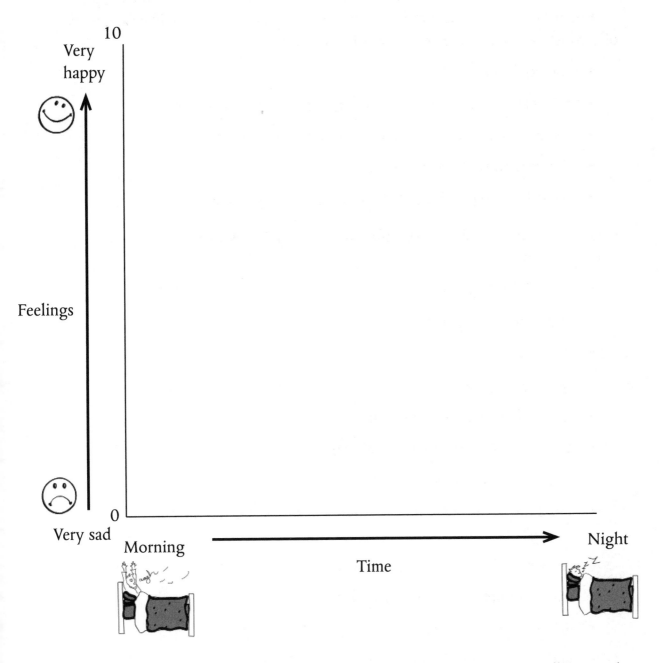

Think about key moments – for example, the crime, telling parents, talking with a friend.

Name . . . . Date . . . .

2.4 Crime can tear people apart... and Putting back the pieces

The aim of this exercise is to explore the needs of the young people, and assist them in thinking about what might help their recovery. The exercise is in two parts: 'Crime tears people apart' and 'Putting back the pieces'.

The young people create a jigsaw of their needs in the first part, with the notion of putting the pieces that may have been displaced since their victimization back together again in the second part. See p.51 for further ideas and examples.

When carrying out these exercises, it is worth remembering the five categories of victims' needs identified by Howard Zehr (2002):

- the need to feel safe

- information and answers to their questions; an explanation

- the chance to tell their story and to be acknowledged

- the need to be back in control

- something to put things back in balance – for example, a gift or apology.

Here are some examples of specific questions or issues that a person hurt by crime may have:

- Why did it happen?

- Will it happen again?

- Am I safe?

- Is my family safe?

- Can I get support or counselling?

- Can I get answers to my questions?

- Can I get any compensation?

- Does the person who did it know how it has affected me and my family?

- How can I be reassured that it won't happen again?

- Can I get help to access transport?

- Can I get an explanation of why the offence happened?

- Is there scope for financial compensation?

- Can I secure reassurance from the offender that it won't happen again?

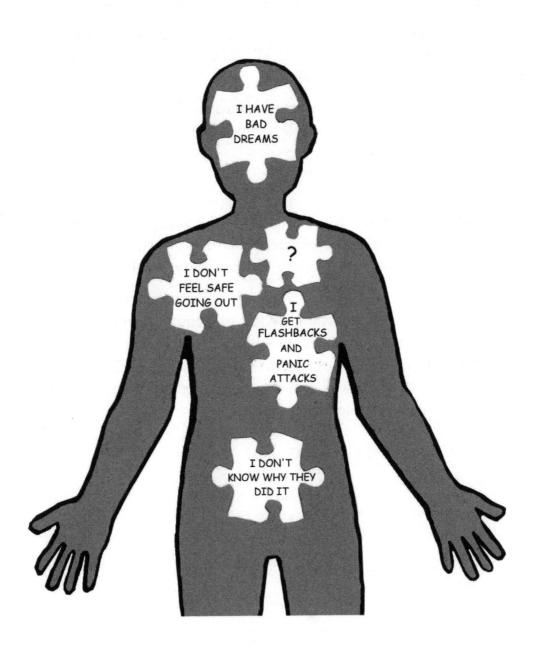

2.4.1 Crime can tear people apart

Instructions

Encourage the young people to come up with a list of four issues or questions that they feel they may need to resolve following what's happened to them.

Ask the young people to write the four issues directly onto the picture inside the jigsaw shapes. Each jigsaw piece shaped hole therefore represents a need.

You could explain to the young people that the jigsaw shapes only cover parts of the body to indicate that the experience of victimization may not have had an impact on every aspect of their life.

Point out to the young people that the outline includes one small shape too many. This is because it may not be possible to repair all the harm caused by the offence.

Tips

- You could discuss where in their body the young people might feel the need (e.g. anxiety might be felt in the stomach, fear in the heart, questions in the head… These are their early warning signs)

- Jenga blocks could be used instead of the jigsaw activity sheets. Start with a tower. Ask the young people to identify the issues or questions that they need to resolve; for each issue, they should remove a block and write the issue on a sticky label. Attach a second label; the young person should write on their idea of what might help them, then carefully replace the block into the tower.

CRIME CAN TEAR PEOPLE APART...

Label each missing jigsaw piece shaped hole, list things you might need to sort out as a result of what happened.

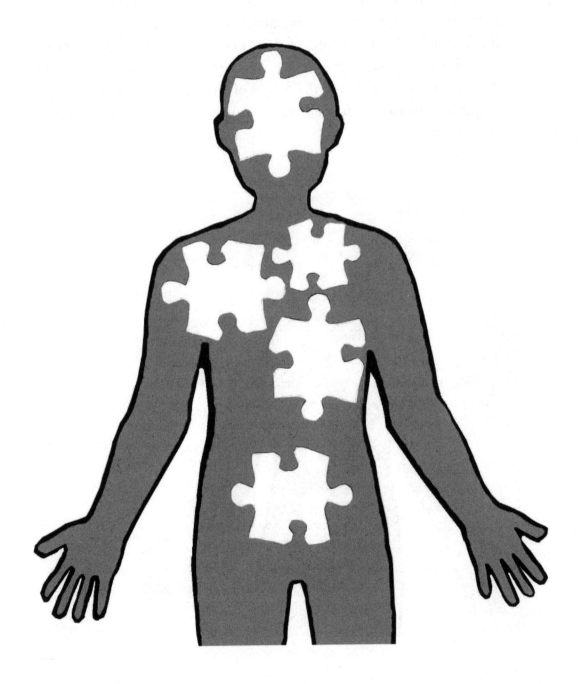

Name . . . . Date . . . .

2.4.2 Putting back the pieces

This exercise follows on from 2.4.1 Crime can tear people apart… See pp.52–53 for further ideas and examples.

Instructions

- The young people now cut out the four jigsaw shapes on p.55 to give them the 'pieces' that will go over the 'holes' to complete their jigsaw.

- Ask the young people to consider something that could be done that might help resolve each of their questions or needs. Every time they think of a resolution for one of their needs, they can write the answer onto the appropriate jigsaw piece, and slot it into the correct place on the outline on p.53. Stress that some of the 'answers' will be things they might be able to do and that you (or someone else) might be able to help them with.

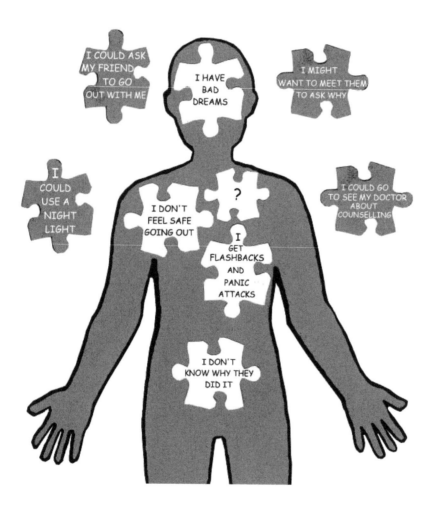

See the illustration above as an example of 'resolution' pieces that will go over the 'needs' holes to complete the jigsaw.

PUTTING BACK THE PIECES

Write down on the pieces ideas about what might help you with your needs. Cut them out and place over the holes to complete your jigsaw.

Name . . . . Date . . . .

2.5 The blob tree

Many young people find it hard to talk about how they're feeling. Sometimes it's easier to look at someone else and say if we feel the same as they look. The blobs on the Blob Tree can be used to help young people explain how they might be feeling.

Instructions

Invite the young person to look at the different blobs on the blob tree. Which one would you be right now? Where would you have been at the time of the incident? Which blob would you like to be? You may like to colour in the blobs that you choose.

Tips

- You may like to provide different coloured crayons and suggest that the young person may like to colour in the blob or blobs that they identify with.

- The blob tree can be useful to support young people in describing a cycle of events – for example, bullying. It can also assist them in recognizing who is available to help them in their recovery.

- Avoid offering your own interpretation for their choice.

THE BLOB TREE

Name . . . . Date . . . .

2.6 Feelings thermometer

When faced with challenging and difficult situations, we all have a unique way of responding. This exercise provides young people with the opportunity to explore their own potential responses, recognizing any early warning signs in their bodies that they may have. It also considers various potential strategies that may be useful to prevent a young person feeling out of control. The illustration below is an example of how a completed exercise sheet might look.

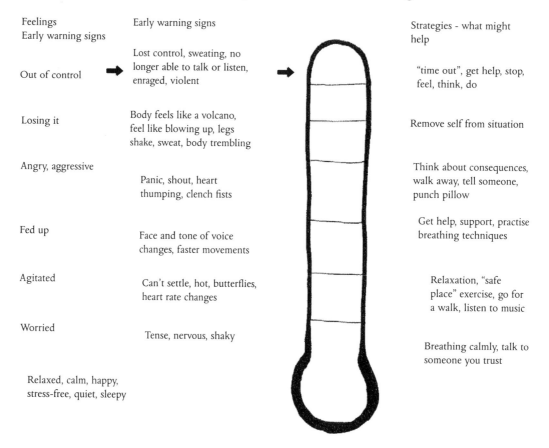

Feelings
Early warning signs

Out of control ➡ Lost control, sweating, no longer able to talk or listen, enraged, violent ➡

Losing it — Body feels like a volcano, feel like blowing up, legs shake, sweat, body trembling

Angry, aggressive

Panic, shout, heart thumping, clench fists

Fed up

Face and tone of voice changes, faster movements

Agitated

Can't settle, hot, butterflies, heart rate changes

Worried

Tense, nervous, shaky

Relaxed, calm, happy, stress-free, quiet, sleepy

Early warning signs

Strategies - what might help

"time out", get help, stop, feel, think, do

Remove self from situation

Think about consequences, walk away, tell someone, punch pillow

Get help, support, practise breathing techniques

Relaxation, "safe place" exercise, go for a walk, listen to music

Breathing calmly, talk to someone you trust

Instructions

Ask the young people to consider a situation where they may experience early warning signs. At each stage of describing the situation, ask them to write on one side of the thermometer what they might be feeling and how they might be behaving, using their own words to describe this. On the other side of the thermometer, ask them to consider what strategies might help. They may want to use different colours to colour in each stage.

Tips

- It is important when completing this exercise with young people to acknowledge that during incidents of crime any control that they may have of the given situation can often be taken away from them however, feelings are feelings; behaviour is a choice and always has an effect.

✓

FEELINGS THERMOMETER

Think of a situation where you might experience your early warning signs. Think about how you might be feeling and behaving before the situation, how you might be feeling and behaving when the situation starts, and how you might be feeling and behaving if the situation continues. Mark this on the left side of the thermometer. On the other side, write down what might help. Think about different things that you might be able to use to help at each stage of the situation that you described. You may want to use different colours to colour in each stage.

Feelings   Early warning signs   Strategies
Out of control   What might help

Calm, relaxed, happy,
stress-free, quiet, sleepy

Name . . . . Date . . . .

2.7 A letter to the person who hurt me

This exercise supports young people in expressing what they might like to say to the person who hurt them.

Sometimes it may be possible for letters to be exchanged or for a direct meeting to be arranged between the different parties in a conflict. This can be powerful and beneficial for everyone. However, this is sensitive work and has to be fully voluntary on all sides. Consider whether there may be a restorative justice worker who can help to facilitate this process, or seek training in restorative practices for yourself.

It may be that the person responsible for the incident is unwilling to communicate. In such circumstances it can be helpful to role play a pretend meeting or for the young people to write a letter to the person who hurt them even if they know that it won't be sent. Burning it or burying it afterwards might be helpful in terms of releasing or clearing some of the feelings that a young person may have.

Instructions

This exercise is more personal and can be more meaningful if the letter is hand-written by the young people, so provide them with suitable writing materials.

Ask them to think about how they would like to address the person (do they know their name?) and then to think about how they are going to start the letter. It might be useful to start the letter by explaining why they are writing it, before then explaining how they have felt since the incident and how they (and maybe others close to them) have been affected.

It may be that the young people would like to include writing down their hopes for the person who hurt them, and perhaps mention something that they hope for themselves or that they are currently doing which is positive.

As an alternative (particularly if there are literacy issues), you may wish to ask the young people to think about what they would like to write to the person who hurt them, and then assist them in expressing this on paper.

Tips

- Facilitating direct or indirect contact between young people and the people who hurt them requires sensitivity and careful preparation. Ask yourself if this is something you can do or if you know any trained other people who can, before discussing this with the young people.

- Letters should never be sent by post.

- When completing this exercise with young people, discuss with them what they would like to do with the letter while being clear about what is possible.

- If the young people choose to burn or bury the letter, ensure you are in a safe environment to do this!

A LETTER TO THE PERSON WHO HURT ME

Write a letter to the person who hurt you. Think about all the things that you would like to say to them and write them down.

Name . . . . Date . . . .

2.8 Strengths checklist

Reminding young people of the strengths and personal qualities that they have, and the achievements that they have made in their life, is important in supporting them in their recovery. Recognizing that people do not usually resolve their difficulties by drawing on their deficits is essential. Young people can be supported in 'moving on' by remembering and using their inner resources and abilities.

Instructions

Suggest in the first instance that the young people draw their own big star like the one shown above. On each point of their star ask them to write a strength, personal quality or achievement that they recognize in themselves.

If this is difficult for some young people, it can be helpful to ask them what strengths others (e.g. their parent or teacher) recognize that they have.

Following on from this, or if the young people are unable to think of anything to put on the points of their star, give them the strengths checklist. Ask them to place a tick in the star that relates to a quality that they recognize they have.

Ask them to draw on their own stars to indicate qualities they may have that aren't already mentioned.

Tips

- Confidence and self-esteem exercises can be a useful way to end sessions or to give as 'take-away' tasks.

- You can use this exercise to point out the strengths that you have noticed in the young person.

✓

STRENGTHS CHECKLIST

Tick any of the stars that apply to you and add any others you can think of.

☆ Making things   ☆ Thinking up new ideas

     ☆ Solving problems   ☆ Cooking

                                                          ☆ Reading

          ☆ Using numbers

                                    ☆ Sport

     ☆ Listening

          ☆ Using my imagination   ☆ Courage

☆ Spelling

          ☆ Dancing

                              ☆ Helping others

     ☆ Trustworthiness

                         ☆ Meeting new people

☆ Occupying myself

          ☆ Sense of humour

Name . . . . Date . . . .

2.9 Growing happy feelings

This exercise encourages young people to think about happiness and things that can help them to feel happy! Flowers usually need a lot of looking after to help them be at their best. Different flowers need different sorts of earth. Some like shade and some like lots of sun. Some will only grow where it is very watery and some like it to be quite dry. In the same way, different people like different things to help them grow happy feelings.

Instructions

Ask young people to imagine that they can grow happy feelings just like you can grow flowers.

Ask them to write down the things that they may need for their own happy feelings to grow. They may like to colour in the flower.

Tips

- Ask the young people to draw their own flower or image that may represent happiness to them.

- Use brightly coloured pens, paints or other craft materials to create the drawing.

- Give the young people their picture with their words on it and suggest that they may want to display it at home to remind them of their happy feelings.

Adapted from Plummer, D. (2007) *Helping Children to Build Self-Esteem* (2nd ed.)
London: Jessica Kingsley Publishers.

GROWING HAPPY FEELINGS

Write down in each petal of the flower the things you need for your happy feelings to grow. You may also like to use your favourite colours to colour in the picture.

Name . . . . Date . . . .

2.10 Unwritten rules

In every aspect of life there are rules that affect our behaviour. (see p.19) Many are written down – the law, health and safety regulations. There are also many rules that influence our behaviour but are not written down. They are expectations that other people put on us and that we put on ourselves. They act as a guide to social interaction and many of them can be very helpful, but sometimes not. These are what we call the 'unwritten rules of society'. We may not believe them or agree with them, but they can still affect our behaviour – for example, 'Boys don't cry', 'Girls wear pink', 'You never grass'.

Supporting young people in completing this exercise may help them to identify unwritten rules that might be holding them back when, for example, they may need to take action for their own safety.

Instructions

Introduce the concept of unwritten rules to young people by discussing with them in a general way what some might be. Provide them with some examples like the ones mentioned here if they are unable to think of any themselves.

Then ask them to think of any unwritten rules that may be directly affecting them. Use the grid on the following page to explore these. How might they be holding them back?

How do they know when they are operating?

What can they do, or what steps might they like to take to overcome resistance to change?

Tips

- Some young people may, from completing this exercise, state that if they don't follow unwritten rules they may feel inadequate and be ostracized or bullied – for example, for not having the right clothing or image. This might hold them back from achieving their full potential or getting the most out of life (e.g. 'Boys don't do ballet.')

- It is therefore important, as supporters, to assist the young people in recognizing when an unhelpful unwritten rule is operating and encourage their confidence to challenge it and take action to ensure their safety.

✓

UNWRITTEN RULES

- Ask yourself the following questions and use the grid to work through your answers.

- What are the unwritten rules that might be holding me back from achieving my full potential?

- How can I recognize when they are affecting me?

- What can I do – what steps can I take – to overcome resistance to change?

Unwritten rule	How do I recognize it?	What can I do?

Name . . . . Date . . . .

Module 3:
Moving on

3.1 My personal support network

This exercise enables young people to think about whom they might turn to when they don't feel safe, if they feel their early warning signs. It can be used to emphasize one of the key themes of protective behaviours: *There is nothing so awful or small that we cannot talk about it with someone.*

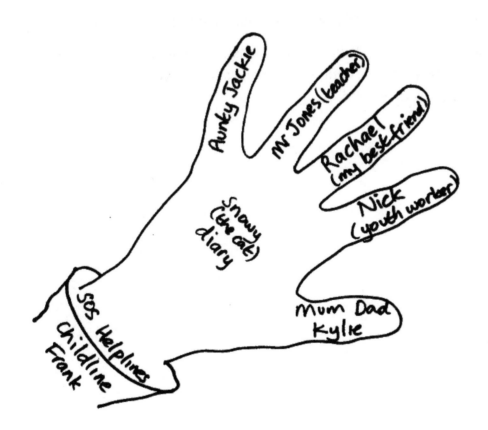

Instructions

Invite the young person to identify their own support network – people they can go to if they have a problem or need to discuss an issue.

Use the activity sheet to explain the idea of creating a support network.

Ask the young person what special qualities they look for in someone to talk to – for example, a good listener, has time, believes you.

Tips

- The hand is something we always have with us so can be a useful reminder of our support network. However, if the young person prefers, their image can be a star, flower or anything they choose.

- The young person may struggle to identify people in their support network. If five fingers are not filled, encourage the young people to be on the look out for new people to add to their network.

- Never tell the young people whom to put on their network, although you can help them in their thinking – for example, is there a particular teacher at school?

- It's important to regularly review support networks as situations change.

- Examples of individuals or organizations to contact in an emergency might be the police or Childline – make sure the young people have the contact details they need.

MY PERSONAL SUPPORT NETWORK

We can all have a helping hand of people to talk with when we do not feel safe. You can make your own helping hand!

- In the space below draw around your hand.

- On each finger, write the name of someone you have on your support network.

- In order to save space you may want to place all the adults who live with you at home on the thumb.

- On the palm of your hand, you can put the name of sources of support which aren't actually people – for example, your pet, teddy bear, diary.

- Up your sleeve you can put the names of people or organizations that you could contact in an emergency e.g. helplines and websites (Childline, Frank, Samaritans), police, social services.

- You may like to have a friends support network on one hand and an adult network on a different diagram.

- You may need to review your network from time to time to make sure the people you have chosen are up to the job!

We need to make decisions *for* ourselves…but…we do not need to make them *by* ourselves…

Name . . . . Date . . . .

3.2 Risking for a purpose

This exercise can assist young people in identifying the steps they can take to get their life back on the track they want, following what has happened to them. For many young people, this may involve confronting some of the fears that they may have gained from their experiences of being victimized, and taking 'risks for a purpose'. A risk for a purpose may be to leave the house on their own, for example, to revisit the site where the incident happened or to go back to sleeping in their own room.

Instructions

Ask the young people to identify the step that they would like to take and to write it in the centre of the footprint.

In each of the toes, ask them to write in the name of something or someone to support them in taking their step.

Outside the footprint, ask the young people to write what the purpose of taking the step is and the benefits that taking it may have for them.

Tips

- It is important to remember that taking a risk for a purpose is something that young people choose to do as a means of moving on in their lives. Care and sensitivity are required by the support worker regarding the timing and appropriateness of introducing this exercise.

- It may be that the young people identify several steps that they need to take, in which case several footprints can be completed.

- Remember to review the steps taken by the young people in follow-up meetings with them. Ask them if they noticed any early warning signs when they were taking their steps and, if so, how they dealt with them.

RISKING FOR A PURPOSE

Think about the step that you are ready to take and write it in the centre of the footprint. On each of the toes, write the name of something or someone who will help you in taking that step. Use the space on the outside of the footprint to write what the purpose of taking the step is, and the benefits that taking it will have for you.

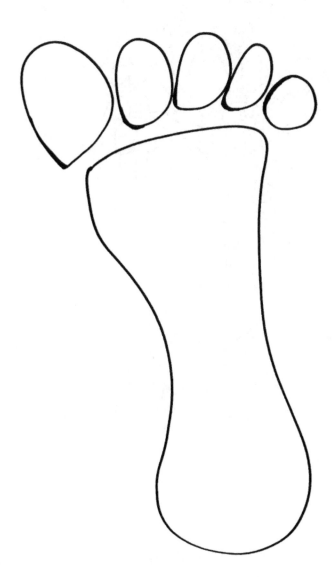

Name . . . . Date . . . .

3.3 My harmony tree

This exercise can be used to support young people in reviewing the progress that they have made. The roots symbolize the support that they have, the trunk symbolizes the positive thing that they have achieved, and the leaves symbolize the effect that this has had for themselves and others.

Instructions

Encourage the young people to draw the trunk of a tree and write one sentence in or next to it to describe something in their life that they have done that is really positive. It could be something like 'going back to school' or 'going to the shop on my own'.

Ask them to draw roots for the tree and write one thing that helped them to make the positive change happen in each root.

Next they should draw leaves and in each leaf write how that positive change has affected themselves and others.

Tips

- The young people may like to choose something significant that they are working towards, rather than something that they have done.

- The harmony tree could be turned into a work of art to remind the young people of what they have achieved.

✓

MY HARMONY TREE

Use the picture on this page as an example to help you draw your own tree. On a blank piece of paper, draw the trunk of a tree and write one sentence in or next to it to describe something you have done that is really positive. Draw the roots of the tree. In each root write one thing that helped you to make the positive change happen. Next draw the leaves. In each leaf, write how the positive change has affected yourself and others.

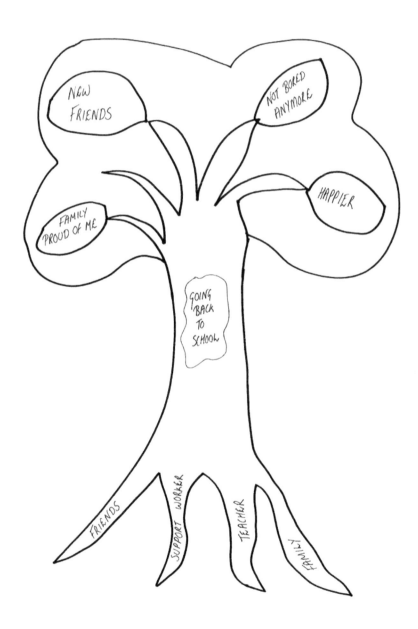

Name . . . . Date . . . .

3.4 A letter to myself

This exercise helps reinforce young people's strategies and strengths. It encourages the young people to reflect on what they are achieving, and how they are able to cope, and offer themselves wise advice.

Instructions

Use the activity sheet to explain the idea of writing a letter from the future.

Suggest that the young people may want to remind themselves of things they can do if they experience any 'Early Warning Signs' in order to help them feel safe.

They may want to include the personal qualities that they have and the strategies that they have learnt.

Tips

- You may want to agree to post the letter to the young people at regular intervals as a helpful reminder!

- It would be better still if the young people addressed it and sent it to themselves.

A LETTER TO MYSELF

Take some time to write a special letter to yourself from the future.

Name . . . . Date . . . .

3.5 Positive self-talk

This exercise supports young people in being able to identify for themselves their qualities and achievements. It may be that they have successfully taken a 'risk for a purpose'. Being able to recognize and mark their inner strengths may positively bolster their self-esteem and support them in continuing in taking steps to aid their recovery.

Instructions

Ask the young people to complete the statements in the boxes and to fill in the blank boxes with positive statements they would like to say to themselves.

Tips

- This exercise may be difficult for some young people to complete.

- If answers are not free-flowing offer some suggestions – for example, 'I did that really well', 'I deserve a medal for keeping cool like that', 'I'm proud of myself'.

- Suggest to the young people that they might want to remind themselves of at least one of their positive self-talk statements every morning.

✓

POSITIVE SELF-TALK

Complete the sentence in each of the boxes. Fill in the blank boxes with positive things you would like to say to yourself.

I am…

I feel positive about…

I have…

I'm proud of…

I feel great from having…

I can…

Name . . . . Date . . . .

3.6 What has changed?

This exercise considers what has changed for the young people as a result of the crime, which is depicted as a wave. Waves wash new things up – some unwelcome. They bring change to the landscape so that things can be different. They also uncover things we didn't realize were there – perhaps things that wouldn't have been revealed without the wave.

Instructions

Encourage the young people to think about things that have changed in their life as a result of the crime. They can draw a pebble for each thing, and label it, or simply talk about it. If they like they can draw any other object they like – things that might be washed up by a large wave, or uncovered from beneath the sand (an old boot, a starfish, a bottle with a message…).

As an alternative, you could bring some pebbles (or other objects) and ask the young person to select them one at a time and lay them on the picture, talking about each in turn and what change it represents.

You could ask: What has the crime uncovered about you? About your family? About your friends?

Tips

- Don't rush in to suggest that there may be positive as well as negative consequences of the crime – many young people will come to this realization themselves.

- Don't analyse their choices for them.

- If appropriate, you can extend the wave imagery – has the wave completely gone? How will it be if another wave comes?

WHAT HAS CHANGED?

- The picture is a beach after a big wave has changed things.
- Draw a pebble for each thing that's changed.
- Write next to it what is different now.
- Has the wave brought anything new?
- Has it uncovered things that were there before, but hidden?

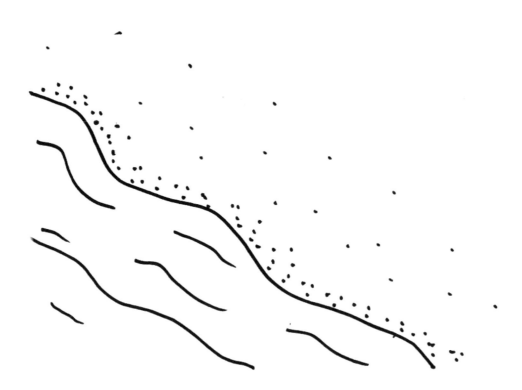

Name . . . . Date . . . .

3.7 The dream catcher

Making a dream catcher can be fun and helpful for young people disturbed by bad dreams. There are many Native American myths that speak of the dream catcher. It is believed that the night air is filled with dreams, both good and bad. The Ojibway tribe believed that good dreams were the source of all wisdom. One tradition was to hang dream catchers throughout their homes. As the dream catcher moves freely in the air, it catches the dreams as they float by. Good dreams know the way and slip through the centre hole, before sliding down off the soft feather so gently that many times the sleeper doesn't know they are dreaming. The bad dreams, not knowing the way, get entangled in the web where they evaporate in the morning sun of the new day.

Instructions

There are many different stories relating to dream catchers. Ask the young people if they know of any, if they would like to make one up, or read with them the Legend of the Ojibway (see Non-book resources).

Schedule a time with the young people to make the dream catcher, and ask them to look out for any feathers, beads, string that they may want to use.

Follow the step-by-step instructions on the following pages.

Tips

- Practise making your own dream catcher before doing this exercise with a young person.

- Ensure that you have scheduled enough time to complete this exercise with a young person; depending on the size of your dream catcher, this can take hours!

- This can be a good exercise to complete on your final session with a young person.

- If you have the time please look at the Legend of Ojibway website mentioned previously for more background information.

THE DREAM CATCHER

1. First find or make yourself a rigid hoop. Long, thin willow brances are free and easily available. Ready-made ones are available in either wood or metal in craft shops at very low cost. Alternatively you might be able to recycle something from a bicycle wheel or plastic containers – use your imagination.

2. Next choose your twine for the web. Traditional dream catchers, made by Native Americans, use sinew or fibre but this is not very easy to source. Waxed cotton is very good, or nylon threads or green garden twine. Garden twine or string is the easiest to use if you want to hang your dream catcher outdoors. You can get metallic threads that are very beautiful but choose something with some grip and not too slippery because this will be easier to work with.

3. To start weaving, take a length of twine at least six times the circumference of your circle. Tie one end of it securely to the circle then scrumple the rest, leaving a workable amount of slack into a ball to make it more manageable.

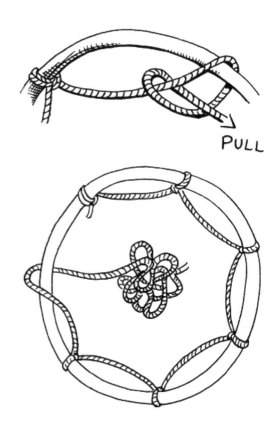

PULL

4. Next loop the thread over the outside of the circle about a sixth of the way around the circumference. Bring it back through the centre, then over where it has come from (through the loop); bring it back to the front and pull taut but not tight. Repeat this all the way around the edge of the circle.

5. To make the web, repeat these same steps but, instead of wrapping the twine around the circle, loop it through the centre of each side of the polygon and so on, spiralling into the middle. As you get smaller in the centre, leave the loops looser.

6. When your thread is nearly finished or as you get close to the centre, gather all your loops by threading your twine just once through each (still following the direction of the spiral pattern).

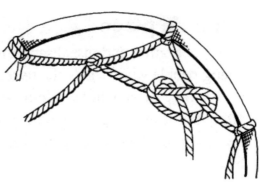

7. Slowly pull the end of the thread, drawing the loops into the centre until they are taut or meet in the middle.

8. Loop the thread around itself and tie it off.

Decorating your dream catcher

- You can attach beads or feathers to any remaining thread hanging from the centre.

- You can also thread beads onto your twine as you weave the web – the Native Americans used beads to represent Iktome the spider who was the keeper of dreams.

- You can also tie feathers or special objects either onto the web, around the circle or dangling underneath on special threads. To add the special threads, take twice the length you require, fold in two, thread the centre through the catcher (at the edge), then thread the other two ends through the centre loop, pulling tight. Tie objects onto the ends.

Name . . . . Date . . . .

3.8 Safe place

Using relaxation and visualisation techniques can be very helpful in reminding young people what it *feels* like to feel safe. This can boost confidence to respond to a variety of situations calmly and rationally. It certainly does not *guarantee* safety but it may support young people in being able to take risks that may be necessary for their development and enjoyment of life without being paralysed by fear.

Instructions

Ask the young people to make themselves comfortable either on a chair or lying down on the floor – whatever feels most relaxed and safe for them.

Suggest that they might find it helpful to close their eyes or alternatively concentrate on a fixed point in the room.

Remind them that they don't have to take part in the exercise and that they have a choice.

Read gently through the suggested script on the following page.

Tips

- Only try this exercise if you have established a supportive working relationship and working environment with the young people.

- Ask the young people if they would like to try this exercise but be clear that they don't have to if they don't want to.

- Before completing this exercise with a young person, try leading it with someone you know to ensure you feel comfortable.

Suggested script

In a moment I am going to ask you to remember, or imagine, a special place, somewhere you can feel or have felt safe. It's okay if you can't think of or remember a safe place; this could be an opportunity to start imagining one.

Take a few deep breaths:

- Breathe out the tension in your body [pause].

- Breathe in relaxation [pause].

- Breathe out the tension [pause].

- Breathe in relaxation [pause].

When you are relaxed, imagine yourself moving towards this place that feels very special and safe to you. You are encouraged by those who love you to visit this wonderful place and experience the feelings of safety. The temperature is just right for you… You feel relaxed and comfortable… You have control.

Imagine yourself in this safe place [silently and slowly count to 20]…

See the colours [silently and slowly count to 10]…

Smell the smells in this safe place [count to 10 again]…

Listen to the sounds [count]…

Taste the tastes [count]…

What can you touch [count]…

Be aware of how you *feel* in this safe place [count]…

If your eyes are closed, keep them closed and, when you are ready, come back into this room, just with your ears, and notice a sound you hadn't heard before…

Now go back to your safe place [count]…

Notice how you feel when you return [count]…

See the colours [count]…

Smell the smells [count]…

Listen to the sounds [count]…

Taste the tastes [count]…

Now choose one of these images to remind you of your safe place. It may be a colour, a sound, a smell or a taste. Associate this image with feeling safe. With practice you could return to this safe place any time you want…

Now when you are ready, come back into this room again just with your ears, hear the sounds… [pause]

Then wriggle your toes and feel your feet on the floor. Now think again of the image you have chosen as your safe place and quickly go back there, to that place where you feel safe and comfortable where you can make decisions calmly. Enjoy this feeling for a few moments… [pause]

Now come back again into this room, first with your ears and when you are ready open your eyes if they have been closed and make a big smile.

How do you *feel* in this safe place?

Could you go back there by remembering the image of your safe place?

Section III: Further Resources

Examples of the exercises in practice

The examples given here demonstrate how some of the exercises have been used to support young people and aid them in their recovery. It is important to note that while summaries of the crimes or incidents that the young people have been subjected to have been included, the sequence of exercises or methods used are not prescriptive or particular to the type of incident. They are tailored to the young people and their experience of what has happened to them.

Case study – Tracey

Tracey had been the subject of harassment and bullying from a neighbouring family for a prolonged period. The mediation service and the police had been involved but Tracey was left feeling fearful and unsafe.

Session	Exercises and activities	Page nos.	Details
1	• Getting to know me • Telling it like it was	pp.36–37 pp.40–41	In the initial meeting with Tracey, using the 'Getting to know me' exercise, the following concerns were identified: feelings of being unable to leave the house; feeling unsafe all the time; feeling harassed at work; feeling suicidal; low self-confidence; disrupted sleeping and eating. Following this, the 'Telling it like it was' exercise was used to enable Tracey to fully think through her feelings and thoughts before, during and after the events.
2	• Feelings, thoughts and behaviour	pp.44–47	Tracey completed the 'Feelings, thoughts and behaviour' exercise with the event of 'Being threatened', as the focus. She used this exercise to ultimately identify that her best, most positive option was 'to walk away and be the better person'. Tracey was able to identify a way out of her situation, which over-rode the more negative options that she had also identified, such as suicide. She realized that she was unable to change others' behaviour, but that she could control her own and what she chose to do.

3	• My feelings graph	pp.48–49	Tracey completed some Feelings graphs for the last year and the last five weeks. She recognized that she had managed to achieve a lot even though she had felt so low. From this Tracey identified that the main cause of her depressive mood was her lack of self-confidence. She completed the 'Positive self-talk' exercise and was able to recognize all the reasons she had to be confident.
	• Positive self-talk	pp.79–80	
4	• A letter to myself	pp.77–78	During the fourth meeting Tracey wrote a letter to herself from the future telling herself how she was going to achieve her goals. In the letter Tracey reminded herself of many of the strategies she had learnt. Her support worker agreed to send her a copy of the letter periodically to remind her of these. Over the following weeks Tracey's mood rose significantly and her ability to improve her own life increased, resulting in her ultimately feeling safer and less fearful.

Case study – Kelly

Kelly, aged 18, had her handbag snatched by two strangers. Several months later, she was finding it hard to move on from the incident, and she felt vulnerable and suspicious of the people around her when she was out on her own.

Session	Exercises and activities	Page nos.	Details
1	• Early warning signs • Risking for a purpose	pp.42–43 pp.72–73	The support worker agreed to meet Kelly at a neutral venue because Kelly felt happier meeting away from her home and work. Kelly readily shared her story and was able to express her feelings through freetalk. The support worker gave her lots of reassurance that it can take time to feel safe again after being the victim of a crime. Kelly identified that going out on her own felt like taking a risk. They discussed that going out was a risk worth taking in order to live an independent life. She needed to go out to get to work or to meet her friends. They completed the 'Risking for a purpose' exercise. Kelly drew her early warning signs on a gingerbread person outline. She was able to recognize some clear physical signs that she experienced when she felt unsafe. She recognized that normally these signs were followed by feeling panicky and out of control if she was out on her own. Her support worker asked her to think about what she might do when she felt these signs. Kelly identified that she could take some deep breaths and think about the situation, assessing whether she was in any real danger. She stated that she could also phone a friend or go somewhere that she felt safer.

2	• My personal support network	pp.69–71	During session two, Kelly commented that she had started recognizing times when she felt scared but she was actually quite safe.
	• Feelings, thoughts and behaviour	pp.44–47	She said that she already felt more confident when she needed to go out on her own. She had started developing her own strategies to help her cope with these situations. Her support worker helped her to identify her personal support network, encouraging her to talk to these people about her feelings and agree with key people that she could call them when feeling unsafe. She knew what to look for in people to trust.
			To cement her learning, Kelly's support worker showed her the 'Feelings, thoughts and behaviour' exercise and explained that this could be used to help her make decisions in lots of situations. Kelly explored being out on her own, all the possible feelings and thoughts, and the different possible behaviour choices she might have. Possibilities included not going out, screaming and running when she felt scared, or using her strategies and support network (her clear favourite!).
			Kelly felt she didn't need another support session but knew she could contact her support worker for further sessions if needed.

Case study – Lisa

Lisa, aged 12, had been subject to malicious threats and name calling via email and text. She had reported the incidents to the police and the perpetrators (older pupils from Lisa's school) had been informally warned. Lisa had been invited to a restorative meeting by the school and the police, but she was unwilling to participate. In addition, she had stopped attending school and had applied for a transfer.

Session	Exercises and activities	Page nos.	Details
1	Getting to know me	pp.36–37	An initial meeting was arranged at Lisa's home where freetalk was used to establish her learning style, if she continued to want support and to discuss confidentiality. Lisa discussed and completed the 'Getting to know me' questionnaire. While not a formal assessment tool, the questionnaire was used to identify potential areas in which Lisa may require support, any areas of immediate concern and a general 'snapshot' of other aspects of her life. In discussing her answers, it was established that Lisa was competent in reading and writing, and also in communicating verbally. In addition she enjoyed art and creative activities. She volunteered some information regarding the incidents that had happened and confirmed that she was unwilling to return to school or participate in a restorative meeting. Lisa was asked what her best hopes from the meeting with a support worker were. She hoped that she would be given support to get her life back to the way it was before the incidents, which involved going out on her own without feeling scared, and regaining confidence and belief in herself. She said she felt safe and comfortable when meeting her worker at home, and that she would like the meetings to continue.

2	• Telling it like it was	pp.40–41	The 'Telling it like it was' exercise was used, focusing on Lisa's feelings and thoughts surrounding what had happened and how she felt now. Lisa used coloured pens and a large piece of paper to draw and write her own version of the exercise. She identified that she was no longer able to sleep well. Her support worker told her the story of the dream catcher and discussed with her what things she might find helpful to try and focus on when trying to go to sleep. She was invited to make a dream catcher with her support worker and, because she was keen to do this, it was agreed that they would make one on their last meeting with each other. Lisa was left with the 'Positive self-talk' exercise to complete if she wanted to prior to the next session.
	• Dream catcher	pp.83–85	
	• Positive self-talk ('take-away' task)	pp.79–80	
3	• Review	p.26	Lisa's support worker started their third meeting by discussing the 'Positive self-talk' exercise and recapping on the previous session. Some of the feelings Lisa had described during the previous session led to the completion of the 'Early warning signs' exercise. Lisa was able to relate some of these feelings to when she thought about going out on her own. This led to the introduction of the 'My personal support network' exercise. Lisa was left with the 'Growing happy feelings' exercise to complete if she wanted, prior to the next session.
	• Early warning signs	pp.42–43	
	• My personal support network	pp.69–71	
	• Growing happy feelings ('take-away' task)	pp.65–66	

| 4 | • Risking for a purpose | pp.72–73 | Lisa had completed the 'Growing happy feelings' exercise. Discussing this was used to commence this session and also to review any outstanding areas that needed to be addressed. The focus of the fourth session was to complete the 'Risking for a purpose' exercise. Lisa used the step 'going out on her own'. She informed the support worker that a new school place had been found for her. |
| 5 | • Feelings, thoughts and behaviour
• Dream catcher | pp.44–47

pp.83–85 | The 'Feelings, thoughts and behaviour' exercise was used for Lisa to explore issues surrounding starting a new school. She identified strategies she was going to use, and reflected on the positive qualities that she recognized within herself.
A review of the sessions completed took place, followed by the making of a dream catcher as a means of ending the sessions. |

Case study – Ashley

Ashley, aged 16, was at home when his house was burgled by three men wearing balaclavas and carrying knives and machetes. They knocked on the front door and when Ashley's father opened it they burst in, demanding cash and valuables. Ashley and his parents were threatened, although they weren't hurt. The burglars weren't caught.

Session	Exercises and activities	Page nos.	Details
1			The sessions were held at Ashley's house and during the first session his support worker introduced himself, explained the nature of the support that could be provided and negotiated boundaries, including confidentiality.

2	• Restorative approach	pp.20–21	The support worker used a restorative approach to enable Ashley to talk freely about the burglary, his feelings and thoughts at the time and how he had been since. The first protective behaviours theme was introduced and discussed. Ashley did the 'Early warning signs' exercise and talked about the early warning signs he had experienced during the incident.
	• Protective behaviours theme	pp.16–20	
	• Early warning signs	pp.42–43	
3	• Review	p.26	Following a review of the previous session, the second protective behaviours theme was introduced, followed by the 'My personal support network' exercise. Ashley was encouraged to identify the qualities he appreciated in the people in his support network, and reflect on whether he had the same qualities in himself and was able to be there for his friends in their times of need.
	• Protective behaviours theme	pp.16–20	
	• My personal support network	pp.69–71	
4	• Feelings, thoughts and behaviours	pp.44–47	On reviewing how things had been since the previous session, Ashley shared experiencing a flashback. This led to a discussion of the early warning signs that the flashback had brought on, and then to a 'Feelings, thoughts and behaviour' exercise to identify Ashley's choices and strategies should a flashback happen again.
5	• Risk for a purpose	pp.72–73	Ashley mentioned that he had chosen to 'Risk for a purpose' by putting himself into the same situation that had triggered the previous flashback, but by using his support network he had felt safe. The session ended by reviewing the incident through the 'What has changed?' exercise, and Ashley was able to reflect on some positive consequences of the burglary, such as his family becoming closer, knowing who his friends were and feeling stronger in himself. My harmony tree was the final exercise to identify something Ashley was excited about to look forward to.
	• What has changed?	pp.81–82	
	• My harmony tree	pp.74–76	

Guidance and tools for using the DVD

The DVD that accompanies this resource was produced by Jo Elliot from Moving Target Films in conjunction with the Oxfordshire Young Victims of Crime Project. The young people in the film are not actors. They are young people who have been hurt by crime and victimization. They volunteered to help make this film by sharing their experiences as a means of helping others. It is therefore with their kind permission that the making of this film has been possible, and sincere thanks go to them for their openness and genuine willingness to 'give'.

The purpose of the DVD is to provide learning material for any adult or peer mentor who may be in a position to offer their support to a young person who has been the victim of crime or victimization. The focus of the DVD is to support the written materials contained within this resource, offering additional insight into their use and application.

However, the DVD can also be used in a broader way by individuals, organizations and groups as a means of:

- raising awareness of the issues affecting young people who have been victims of crime

- highlighting the necessity for appropriate support to be available to address the needs of such young people

- demonstrating diversity and the importance of treating young people as individuals, with their individual experience as the starting point for intervention.

The DVD is also suitable for use in youth groups, school assemblies and citizenship lessons etc. If being shown directly to young people, ensure that you have watched the whole of the film yourself first. Some young people may find some of the contents distressing or be frightened by what they hear. Others may glamourize or try to diminish what they see. Select the section of the DVD that you want to show according to the amount of time available and the purpose of the session – that is, whether you are catering for needs of an individual or a group of young people.

The DVD has two modules:

- Module 1: 'Crime hurts' features young people sharing their real experiences of being victimized. These include two different incidents of domestic burglary, an assault, an incident of bullying and one case of being the victim of grievous bodily harm.

- Module 2: 'Protective behaviours' provides practical insight into how some of the exercises may be delivered and incorporated into supportive sessions with young people. This module features Penny Bassett, an accredited trainer from Protective Behaviours UK, an organization from which many of the exercises in this resource have been drawn and adapted (www.pennybassett.com).

Expansion activities

In the following pages, we have provided some ideas and inspiration for how the DVD can be used as a springboard for further discussion. The activities can be used for you as practitioner to reflect on your own practice, or with young people. When doing so, you may find it useful to refer back to the information on the experience and effects, both physiological and psychological, of being a victim on pp.26–29 at the beginning of the resource.

When watching the protective behaviours film, which shows a pracitioner working with a young person, consider if it might be helpful to explore the two main protective behaviour themes with the young people you are supporting. You may find that you can use or adapt some of the reflective exercises described here with the young people, though it may not always be appropriate or necessary. When watching the support worker in the film introduce the young person to the activities and engage them, think about how you might do this. What would lead into the introduction of each exercise? How might you end the session? If you were in a position to offer a number of sessions, how might you link each session to the next?

✓

Crime hurts – feelings, thoughts and behaviours

While watching the film, ask yourself the following questions or use the grid below to write down your answers.

What effects do the young people featured in the DVD say that their experiences of crime or victimization has had upon them?		
How have their experiences affected...		
their feelings?	their thoughts?	their behaviour?

Crime hurts – thinking about crime

From the different accounts given by the young people, what crimes have been committed?

Is bullying a crime? What difference does it make?

Crime hurts – thinking about support

What support might some of the young people in the film need?

Think about each of the young people featured in the film. Which exercises contained in this resource might be useful to each of them?

Protective behaviours – feeling safe

The film you have just watched introduces the two main themes of protective behaviours:

- We all have the right to feel safe.

- There is nothing so awful or small that we can't talk about it with someone.

We all have the right to feel safe, but sometimes things happen to us to make us feel unsafe and insecure. Ask yourself the following questions and write down your answers in the table below.

What rights do you think that young people have?

Are the rights of young people the same as adults? What differences might there be?

We all have the right to feel safe all the time and the right to be aware of and to take action at those times when we do not feel safe, when our internal body signals (early warning signs) tell us that all is not well.

With each of our rights there is a responsibility. For example, if I have a right to be treated with respect, I have a responsibility to treat others with respect.

✓

If we all have the right to feel safe, what is our responsibility to others?

'If someone hurts us, we still have a responsibility to respect the rights of others, although it does not give us the right to hurt them back.'
Consider this statement and write your thoughts regarding it in the box below.
Use your answers as a springboard for futher discussion.

Remember!

'We all' is an equal opportunities statement. There are no exceptions.

'All the time' – we have the right at all times even if we can't exercise it.

'Feel safe' – NOT be safe.

I have the right to feel safe and respect that everyone has the same right too.

Protective behaviours – feeling safe

Ask yourself, 'How does safe feel?'

How might an upsetting experience make a difference ot what you think is safe?

When thinking of your answers it might be helpful to consider the suggestions below:

Warm? Cosy? Comfortable? Friendly? Happy? Contented? Being with someone I like or trust?

These are words we often use when talking about feeling safe, but it is also possible to feel safe at other times too, even when we feel cold or sad or angry or alone.

Feeling cold on a winter's day is not an unsafe feeling unless we have no hope of feeling warm again.

Feeling angry is not an unsafe feeling when the reasons for it are understood, when it's right to be angry about something, and if we express ourselves in a way that is appropriate.

There are times when feelings of anger, sadness and discomfort are closely associated with fear, but feeling safe does not always have to be a warm and fuzzy experience. Because most of us are safe most of the time, it can be difficult to describe, because it's an every day experience. It is something many people take for granted.

✓

Protective behaviours – 'There is nothing so awful or so small that we can't talk about it'

Take some time to think about each part of this statement. Write your thoughts in the table below. Some suggestions for your answers are made on the next page.

There is nothing – what does this part of the statement mean to you?

So awful or small – what does this part of the statement mean to you?

We can't talk about it with someone – Ask yourself what it might feel like to talk to someone. What kind of person would they need to be? What qualities would they have?

THERE IS NOTHING	Absolute, it really means nothing!
SO AWFUL OR SMALL	Typical responses include: terrible, secretive, horrible, disgusting. It's important to remember that some young people might feel that their problems are too insignificant compared to others and so might not seek help when they may need it.
WE CAN'T TALK ABOUT IT	What might it feel like to talk to someone who listened? Like a release? A relief? Freedom? Hopeful? Lighter? That it helps to make things clearer?
WITH SOMEONE	What might it feel like to talk to someone who will listen, understand, have compassion, believe us, not judge us, help us explore our options, be willing to take action for us. What kind of a person would they need to be? In cases of absolute emergency, we may need to have to ask the help of a stranger, so it might not always be someone we trust.

Useful Resources

Books

Children's Safety Education Foundation (2007) *A Little Ray of Hope: A Self-Help Guide for the Parents of Child Victims.* Stockport: Children's Safety Education Foundation.

Coleman, J. and Brooks, F. (2009) *Key Data on Adolescence.* Young People in Focus.

Connexions (2006) *The Know Yourself Book.* Oxford: Oxfordshire County Council.

Dolan, Y. (2000) *Beyond Survival: Living Well is the Best Revenge.* London: BT Press.

Gilgun, J. (1998) Lemons or Lemonade? *An Anger Workbook for Teens.* Clifton, NJ: Bell Press.

Humphreys, C., Thiara, R., Skamballis, A. and Mullender, A. (2006) *Talking to my Mum: A Picture Workbook for Workers, Mothers and Children Affected by Domestic Abuse.* London: Jessica Kingsley Publishers.

Ironside, V. (2004) *The Huge Bag of Worries.* London: Hodder Children's Books.

McGowan, M. (2002) *Young People and Peer Support.* Brighton: Trust for the Study of Adolescence.

Melia, J. (2005) Wavelength: *A Handbook of Communication Strategies for Working with Young People.* Brighton: Trust for the Study of Adolescence.

Morga, J. and Zedner, L. (1992) *Child Victims: Crime, Impact and Criminal Justice.* Oxford: Oxford University Press.

O'Hanlon, B. and Beadle, S. (2000) *A Field Guide to Possibility Land.* London: BT Press.

Plummer, D. (2005) *Helping Adolescents and Adults to Build Self-Esteem.* London: Jessica Kingsley Publishers.

Plummer, D. (2007) *Helping Children to Build Self-Esteem.* London: Jessica Kingsley Publishers.

Stace, S. and Roker, D. (2006) *Keeping them Safe: Toolkit for People Working with Parents of Young People.* Brighton: Trust for the Study of Adolescence.

Sunderland, M. (2000a) *Helping Children with Low Self Esteem: Guidebook and Children's Book.* Milton Keynes: Speech Mark Publishing.

Sunderland, M. (2000b) *Helping Children who are Anxious or Obsessional: Guidebook and Children's Book.* Milton Keynes: Speech Mark Publishing.

Sunderland, M. (2000c) *Helping Children who Bottle Up their Feelings: Guidebook and Children's Book.* Milton Keynes: Speech Mark Publishing.

Sunderland, M. (2000d) *Helping Children who have Hardened their Hearts and Become Bullies: Guidebook and Children's Book.* Milton Keynes: Speech Mark Publishing.

Sunderland, M. (2003) *Helping Children with Fear: Guidebook and Children's Book.* Milton Keynes: Speech Mark Publishing.

Sunderland, M. and Engleheart, P. (1993) *Draw on Your Emotions.* Milton Keynes: Speech Mark Publishing.

Warren, C. and Williams, S. (2007) *Restoring the Balance 2: Changing Culture through Restorative Approaches.* London: Lewisham Council Restorative Approaches Partnership.

Williams, B. (1999) *Working with Victims of Crime.* London: Jessica Kingsley Publishers.

Williams, B. (ed.) (2002) *Reparation and Victim-Focused Social Work.* London: Jessica Kingsley Publishers.

Williams, B. (2005) *Victims of Crime and Community Justice.* London: Jessica Kingsley Publishers.

Non-book resources

Coleman, J. (2001) *A Little Bit of Respect: What Young People want from Adults* (training video). London: Youth Justice Board.

Devon and Cornwall Constabulary (2008) *Sense of Adventure* (resource cards illustrated by Nick Mussell). Exeter: Devon and Cornwall Constabulary.

Legend of the Ojibway. Available at www.newworldencyclopedia.org/entry/dreamcatcher.

NHS Choices, *Post-traumatic Stress Disorder*. NHS website. Available at www.nhs.uk/conditions/Post-traumatic-stress-disorder/Pages/Introduction.aspx, accessed on 20 July 2010.

Shared Futures: Supporting the Integration of Refugee Children and Young People in School and Wider Community (2008). Includes DVD. London: Salusbury World.

St Luke's Innovative Resources (1996) *Strength Cards for Kids*. Bendigo, VA: Australia: St Luke's Innovative Resources.

Protective Behaviours and Restorative Justice resources

PBUK – Protective Behaviours UK has further information about PBs including training opportunities.

www.protectivebehaviours.co.uk

Penny Bassett – PBUK Trainer

penfriend@pennybassett.com

www.pennybassett.com

Feeling Safe Standing Strong a group work programme based on the PBs process. Penny Bassett and Tim Lee

www.feelingsafestandingstrong.com

NIWAF – Northern Ireland Women's Aid Federation – Helping Hands for Children a resource pack for primary school aged children based on PBs to develop self-esteem and explore feelings, safety and healthy ways to manage conflict.

www.niwaf.org

Incentive Plus – Resources to promote social, emotional and behavioural skills including PBs resources.

www.incentiveplus.co.uk

Restorative Justice Consortium is the umbrella organization for Restorative Approaches in England and Wales, offering information, events, news and resources for those wanting to learn more about restorative approaches as well as support and networking for restorative practitioners and trainers.

www.restorativejustice.org.uk

Transforming Conflict is the national centre for restorative justice in youth settings, offering training, advice, resources, consultancy, plenary speakers and workshop leaders and partnership.

www.transformingconflict.org

The Pocket Guide to Restorative Justice – Wallis, P. and Tudor, B. (2008) London; Jessica Kingsley Publishers. This is a practical, "how to do it" guide for trained restorative practitioners.

References

HM Government (2009) *Youth Crime Action Plan: The Good Practice Guide for Supporting Young Victims of Crime.* London: Home Office.

Wallis, P. (2010) *Are You Okay? A Practical Guide to Helping Young Victims of Crime.* London: Jessica Kingsley Publishers.

Wallis, P. with Aldington, C. and Leibmann, M. (2010) *What Have I Done? A Victim Empathy Programme for Young People.* London: Jessica Kingsley Publishers.

Victim Support (2009) *Youth Victims – the Cost of Crime – Workshop Guidance for Facilitators.* London: Metropolitan Police and the London Criminal Justice Board.

Wood, M. (2005) *The Victimization of Young People: Findings from the Crime and Justice Survey 2003.* London: Home Office.

Zehr, H. (2002) *The Little Book of Restorative Justice.* Intercourse, PA: Good Books (Can be ordered from London Mennonite Centre, tel: 020 8340 8775 or www.menno.org.uk/).